DSST
Ethics in America Exam

SECRETS

Study Guide
Your Key to Exam Success

DSST Test Review for the
Dantes Subject Standardized Tests

Dear Future Exam Success Story:

Congratulations on your purchase of our study guide. Our goal in writing our study guide was to cover the content on the test, as well as provide insight into typical test taking mistakes and how to overcome them.

Standardized tests are a key component of being successful, which only increases the importance of doing well in the high-pressure high-stakes environment of test day. How well you do on this test will have a significant impact on your future, and we have the research and practical advice to help you execute on test day.

The product you're reading now is designed to exploit weaknesses in the test itself, and help you avoid the most common errors test takers frequently make.

How to use this study guide

We don't want to waste your time. Our study guide is fast-paced and fluff-free. We suggest going through it a number of times, as repetition is an important part of learning new information and concepts.

First, read through the study guide completely to get a feel for the content and organization. Read the general success strategies first, and then proceed to the content sections. Each tip has been carefully selected for its effectiveness.

Second, read through the study guide again, and take notes in the margins and highlight those sections where you may have a particular weakness.

Finally, bring the manual with you on test day and study it before the exam begins.

Your success is our success

We would be delighted to hear about your success. Send us an email and tell us your story. Thanks for your business and we wish you continued success.

Sincerely,

Mometrix Test Preparation Team

Need more help? Check out our flashcards at: http://MometrixFlashcards.com/DSST

Copyright © 2015 by Mometrix Media LLC. All rights reserved.
Written and edited by the Mometrix Exam Secrets Test Prep Team
Printed in the United States of America

TABLE OF CONTENTS

Top 20 Test Taking Tips 1
Ethical Traditions 2
Ethical Analysis of Issues and Practical Applications 44
Practice Test 97
    Answers and Explanations 106
Secret Key #1 - Time is Your Greatest Enemy 111
    Pace Yourself 111
Secret Key #2 - Guessing is not Guesswork 111
    Monkeys Take the Test 111
    $5 Challenge 112
Secret Key #3 - Practice Smarter, Not Harder 113
    Success Strategy 113
Secret Key #4 - Prepare, Don't Procrastinate 113
Secret Key #5 - Test Yourself 114
General Strategies 114
Special Report: How to Overcome Test Anxiety 120
    Lack of Preparation 120
    Physical Signals 121
    Nervousness 121
    Study Steps 123
    Helpful Techniques 124
Additional Bonus Material 129

- ii -

Top 20 Test Taking Tips

1. Carefully follow all the test registration procedures
2. Know the test directions, duration, topics, question types, how many questions
3. Setup a flexible study schedule at least 3-4 weeks before test day
4. Study during the time of day you are most alert, relaxed, and stress free
5. Maximize your learning style; visual learner use visual study aids, auditory learner use auditory study aids
6. Focus on your weakest knowledge base
7. Find a study partner to review with and help clarify questions
8. Practice, practice, practice
9. Get a good night's sleep; don't try to cram the night before the test
10. Eat a well balanced meal
11. Know the exact physical location of the testing site; drive the route to the site prior to test day
12. Bring a set of ear plugs; the testing center could be noisy
13. Wear comfortable, loose fitting, layered clothing to the testing center; prepare for it to be either cold or hot during the test
14. Bring at least 2 current forms of ID to the testing center
15. Arrive to the test early; be prepared to wait and be patient
16. Eliminate the obviously wrong answer choices, then guess the first remaining choice
17. Pace yourself; don't rush, but keep working and move on if you get stuck
18. Maintain a positive attitude even if the test is going poorly
19. Keep your first answer unless you are positive it is wrong
20. Check your work, don't make a careless mistake

Ethical Traditions

Socrates

Socrates, a philosopher who lived in ancient Athens, Greece c. 470~469-399 BCE, is known as a major contributor to the foundations of Western philosophy. He fought in the Athenian army in the Potidaea, Amphipolis, and Delium campaigns. A master stonemason by trade, after retirement he only discussed philosophy. An inherent difficulty in knowing many biographical facts about Socrates is that he did not write down anything himself; his student and disciple Plato collected much of what he said in his *Dialogues*. However, due to Plato's admiration of Socrates, much of what he wrote about him is idealized. The comedic playwright Aristophanes was a contemporary and wrote of Socrates, but since his plays were parodies, so was his Socratic character. The great historian Thucydides never mentioned Socrates or other philosophers. Xenophon was the one historian to write about Socrates, and is considered more reliable. Historians commonly combine and try to reconcile texts from these authors to achieve a consistent, if not realistic, account. He is thought to have criticized Athenian democracy following the Peloponnesian Wars, incurring governmental disfavor that could have contributed to his death sentence.

Although Socrates maintained he was a philosopher, not a teacher—even stating in Plato's *Apology* that his poverty was proof he did not accept payment for teaching—he did teach his students, e.g., Plato and Xenophon, a great deal. He developed a dialectic method of teaching whereby instead of telling information or ideas to students, he asked them questions, now called the Socratic dialogue. His questions not only elicited a variety of answers from individual students, they also enabled students to gain important insights into the topics discussed. This practice is now called the Socratic Method—*elenchus* in Greek—and is widely used in teaching. Socrates also contributed significant, enduring development to the discipline of epistemology (the study and theory of knowledge). His philosophical concepts form a basis for the majority of modern Western philosophies. His illustrations of irony have acquired the term Socratic irony. His real-life espousal of ethical principles is reflected in his refusal to defend the status quo and the political "might makes right" philosophy in Athens: he criticized and questioned societal and governmental practices he found immoral, advocating goodness and justice.

After Athens' defeat by Sparta in the Peloponnesian Wars, the city-state sought to recover from this humiliation. Part of this recovery likely involved quelling public misgivings about democratic government. Socrates is thought to have criticized democracy. In several of Plato's dialogues, he praised the Spartans. Socrates vowed loyalty to Athens as his city, including disagreement with its current social and political practices. Plato described Socrates as the "gadfly" of Athens, in that he stung Athenian politicians into action as a gadfly stings horses into movement. The "might makes right" political and military philosophy often demonstrated by Athens and articulated by Thucydides was one Socrates criticized as unethical. Socrates was known for posing paradoxes. His friend Chaerephon reportedly was told by the oracle at Delphi that nobody was wiser than Socrates. Socrates characterized this as a paradox: he believed he had no wisdom. But, questioning members of the populace, he found they knew very little yet believed themselves wise. He declared the oracle correct, saying he was the only one wise enough to recognize his own lack of wisdom. Powerful Athenians, feeling made to appear foolish, accused, tried and executed him.

According to historian Xenophon and philosopher/author Plato, both Socrates' contemporaries, once the Athenian court sentenced him to die for heresy ("not believing in the gods of the state") and corrupting young Athenians' minds, Socrates would have been able to escape execution because his followers could bribe the prison guards. Xenophon wrote that Socrates actually found death preferable to the difficulties of old age. Others also reported Socrates felt it was the "right time" for his death. Scholars speculate several reasons he chose not to escape: he believed no real philosopher fears death and did not want to demonstrate this by fleeing. His questioning and criticism would likely evoke equal disfavor in other countries. He believed he would be breaking his social contract with Athens of agreeing to live by its laws if he were to escape punishment for being found guilty, which would violate his principles. He may also have wanted to avoid making his friends who offered to help him escape legally liable. Socrates' reasons for staying to be executed are the primary topic of Plato's *Crito.*

Socrates is believed to have been sentenced to death by the Athenian judicial system largely for having criticized Athenian democracy and its political and military philosophy, and for having questioned powerful Athenians, publicly making them seem foolish. For example, after interviewing assorted citizens, he announced they thought themselves wise yet knew little, and so declared himself wiser than they for being the only one to realize he knew nothing. Affronted by his embarrassing them thus, they began to accuse him of wrongdoing, such as not believing in the "gods of the state" and corrupting young people's thoughts. At the end of his *Phaedo,* Plato describes Socrates' death. He reports Socrates' last words to Crito being, "Crito, we owe a rooster to Asclepius. Please, don't forget to pay the debt." Asclepius was the Greek god of curing illnesses. Scholars interpret Socrates' statement to mean that death cures the illness of the human condition, and frees the soul from its mortal body. Also, one author (Waterfield, 2009) proposes Socrates sacrificed himself voluntarily to become a cure for Athens' moral and social ills.

Socrates developed a dialectic inquiry method to examine Justice, the Good, and other central moral concepts. He would guide students in problem-solving by breaking the problem down into a series of carefully planned questions. These questions helped students ascertain how much they know and their underlying beliefs. As in deductive reasoning, the questions would successively identify and eliminate contradictory hypotheses until the best hypotheses were discovered. As they gradually arrived at the answer they sought, students were made to examine what they believed and whether or not those beliefs and values were valid or not. This technique is the major influence on today's application of the scientific method, wherein hypotheses are posed, then tested, and then refuted or supported. Some scholars also view Socratic dialectic as a spiritual exercise. They point out Plato's belief that such exercises direct the soul away from the material world and toward the Good. Others describe it as a method for mentally visualizing, intuiting, or revealing the godly, original Ideas, Forms, or Mysteries usually disguised by worldly appearances.

Thucydides

Thucydides lived around 460-395~400 BCE in ancient Athens, Greece. He was a military general, a political philosopher, and preeminently a historian. He became known as the father of scientific history because he adhered to rigorous methods for finding information, using objective evidence, and analyzing it according to causal relationships rather than attributing events to unprovable reasons like actions by the gods, as many other ancient Greeks did. He is also credited with being the father of political realism, a school of philosophy characterizing international relations with the concept "might makes right." His Melian Dialogue is still central to international relations theory. His History of the Peloponnesian War covers this Athens-Sparta war until 411 BCE. While contemporary historians have few details of his biography, Thucydides' history also informs them of his paternity, residence, and nationality; and his having fought in the war, caught the plague, and being exiled. In addition to recounting history, his interests included explaining human behavior during civil wars, massacres, and plagues.

Herodotus, who died roughly 35 years before Thucydides was born, was known as the father of history, while Thucydides was called the father of scientific history. Like many of his time, Herodotus attributed historical events to the wrath of the Greek gods, invoked by misplaced human arrogance. Thucydides, however, excluded intervention by the gods in his historical writing; he was more interested in human behaviors as causes than divine agency. While Herodotus interpreted history as initiated by injustices and maintained through cyclical revenge to provide moral instruction, Thucydides saw the gods as mental fabrications of humans dictated by political needs, and preferred factual accounts and political interpretations. Another difference is that Herodotus wrote more of past history, while Thucydides recorded events contemporary with his own life. In his The Histories, Herodotus presented contradictory and/or improbable stories without judging, letting readers make their own decisions. He included oral fables collected during travel, plus ethnographic and geographic information; Thucydides found these less important.

In his *History of the Peloponnesian War,* Thucydides retells historical events in narrative form. Classical scholars place Thucydides' writing in the same narrative tradition influenced by Hesiod, author of the *Theogamy,* and the great oral poet Homer, who sang the epic tales of the Trojan War and Odysseus in the *Iliad* and the *Odyssey*, respectively. They additionally note the similarity in the way tragedians Aeschylus and Sophocles treated themes of suffering and morality and Thucydides' interest in these themes. Moreover, scholars remark that philosophers Plato and Aristotle dealt with related concepts of misfortune and justice, another influence revealed in Thucydides' history. One scholar (Lebow, 2003) even called Thucydides "the last of the tragedians" because he not only wrote his history in narrative form, but also constructed it by drawing liberally from the aforementioned ancient Greek tragedies and epic poems. Another common characteristic Thucydides' history shares with the epic poems and tragic plays is representing human behavior as the source of human downfall. Thus some interpret his *History* as a warning to future political leaders that, with an objective historian recording them, their actions should show better judgment.

Many scholars believe Thucydides was influenced by the oral narrative tradition of Homer's epic poetry and the dramatic monologues used in plays by tragedians Aeschylus and Sophocles. Most of Thucydides' sources were oral accounts of political and military events from contemporary eyewitnesses. When he set his history in writing, Thucydides not only preserved them for posterity, but also transformed them through his writing style, which used a heroic register. Thucydides himself stated that he did not record what was said verbatim; he wrote what he felt was the gist of what he heard, and moreover what he thought should have been said. For example, Pericles' funeral oration in his history is thought to combine two funeral speeches by Pericles, and commonly accepted to have been edited by Thucydides rather than transcribed word-for-word. This speech has been suggested as an influence on Lincoln's Gettysburg Address: though ten times longer, its structure, themes, and tone can be found in Lincoln's briefer speech. As written, Pericles' oration provides timeless insights into military politics and human behavior.

Thucydides, whose death is estimated at c. 400~395 BCE, conveyed many insights concerning the wars he chronicled. He believed Sparta's initial 430 BCE attack was a preemptive strike motivated by Spartan fear of Athens. Sparta had greater military power and discipline on land, while Athens had greater naval power and the more creative leadership of a democracy. To recount the war's events, Thucydides used a combination of narrative storytelling, speeches crafted as dramatic monologues, and dialogues representing ethical debates about war. For example, Pericles' funeral oration is the history's most famous dramatic speech. The Mytilene Debates emphasize Athenian mercy, even when suppressing revolts; the Melian Dialogue, discussing events only a few years after the Mytilenian revolt, instead emphasizes "might makes right"—when the neutral Melos island inhabitants protested they had done nothing and pled for their lives, Athens responded that its ability to destroy them justified doing so.

Without invoking godly intervention as a cause of human events, Thucydides still managed to show in his history that the 413 BCE defeat of Athens by Sparta in Sicily (prior to Athens' ultimate surrender in 404 BCE, probably after Thucydides' death) was a consequence of near cosmic proportions for the ethical deterioration of Athenian society, as well as the logical result of flawed leadership. In his account of Athens' crushing Melos, which was not involved in the wars, Thucydides popularized the concept of "might makes right" espoused in modern times by Machiavelli ("the end justifies the means") and Bismarck and others in *Realpolitik* (von Rochau's terms for political realism). As Thucydides expressed it in the Melian Dialogue, "Right, as the world goes, is only in question between equals in power." Though today Thucydides' status is as one of the world's greatest historians, this was not the case during his time. Aristotle's works discussing the same periods never mention him several decades after his death.

Roman author Cicero described Thucydides as a great historian by the 1st century BCE; a century later, Lucian credited Thucydides with giving Greek historians their "law" of recording facts. As with most classical literature, his work was lost in Western Europe during Medieval illiteracy, but continued to influence the Byzantine Empire in the East. Following the Renaissance, classical works were revived in the Western world. During the Protestant Reformation, the information Thucydides provided about Middle Eastern countries in his history was used to determine Biblical chronology, as was recommended by physicist Isaac Newton. Thomas Hobbes *(Leviathan)* first translated Thucydides' history into English in 1628. Eighteenth-century historians greatly admired his work. Friedrich Nietzsche and many other 19th-century German philosophers formed a cult that followed Thucydides as a "portrayer of man" and the source of "the most impartial knowledge of the world." Political historians in the 20th century studying long-term economics, cultures, and everyday life patterns were influenced by his work, as were Cold War international relations.

In 55 BCE, the great Roman Cicero wrote in his *De Oratore* that Thucydides, "in my opinion, easily vanquished all in the artfulness of his style." Cicero commented that while Thucydides' information was extensive, he was such a master of compression that "he almost matches the number of... words with the number of... thoughts." He noted Thucydides' mastery of wording so perfectly representing ideas they were inseparable: "so apposite and compressed... you do not know whether his matter is... illuminated by his diction or his words by his thoughts." Translating Thucydides from Greek to English in 1628, Thomas Hobbes named him "the most politic historiographer that ever wrote" in his preface. A century later, David Hume (1742) wrote that the "first page of Thucydides is, in my opinion, the commencement of real history." Nietzsche (1889) found Thucydides a "radical cure... for the lamentably rose-colored idealization of the Greeks." Poet W. H. Auden (1939), writing of World War II, referred to him: "Exiled Thucydides knew/All that a speech can say/About Democracy,/And what dictators do..." and that Thucydides "Analysed all in his book,/The enlightenment driven away,/The habit-forming pain,/Mismanagement and grief:/We must suffer them all again."

Plato

Plato lived in ancient Athens, Greece from c. 428~427 and 424~423-348~347 BCE. He was a mathematician as well as a philosopher. An avid student and disciple of the philosopher Socrates, Plato is best known for writing down the important teachings and ideas of Socrates, which Socrates never did himself. (When written language first developed in Greece, Socrates criticized its arbitrary dissemination, favoring the oral tradition. He may have anticipated that writing could misrepresent some people's ideas and then become permanent, contrasted with the continual evolution of living spoken language. Ironically, his own ideas and words would have been lost to posterity without Plato's writing.) Plato founded Athens' Academy, the Western world's first higher learning institution. He is also famed as the teacher of Aristotle, his best-known student. Plato is credited with Socrates and Aristotle for contributing the bases for Western philosophy and science. The famous modern mathematician and philosopher Alfred North Whitehead (1861-1947) characterized European philosophy as "a series of footnotes to Plato."

Though philosopher Socrates was the most famous influence on Plato, mathematician Pythagoras also significantly influenced him. Pythagoras formed a community in Croton of intellectuals who thought similarly and were strongly organized; scholars (cf. Hare, 1982, 1999) refer to this community as a model for the Platonic Republic. Plato's idea that mathematics and abstract thought are solid foundations for scientific, ethical, and philosophical thinking is believed to have been acquired from Pythagoras. Both Pythagoras and Plato are thought to have been influenced by Orphism, an ancient Greek and Thracian religion based on the myth of Orpheus. Contemporary Aristotle stated that Plato's philosophy adhered closely to Pythagorean principles. Later, the Roman Cicero reiterated this, writing, "They say Plato learned all things Pythagorean." In *A History of Western Philosophy* (1945), Bertrand Russell maintained that Pythagoras' influence on Plato and other philosophers was so strong that Pythagoras should be regarded as the most influential Western philosopher.

Plato's *Dialogues* have been and continue to be used in education to instruct students in subjects that include not only philosophy and logic, but also ethics, religion, mathematics, and rhetoric. Plato's theory of Forms reflected an unusual view of abstract things. This theory developed into the Platonic school of thinking (Platonism). While Plato was Socrates' student, Plato's own student Aristotle contrasted the Socratic vs. Platonic concepts of Forms by saying that examination of the natural world can reveal Socrates' concept of Forms, whereas Plato's conceptualization of Forms is that they exist outside of and beyond the scope of humans' usual understanding. The historian Xenophon and the comedic playwright Aristophanes depicted Socrates differently from the way Plato did. Some authors question the validity of viewing Plato as the spokesperson for Socrates, considering Socrates' known penchant for using irony as well as the naturally dramatic character of the dialogue as a literary format.

While Plato may have idealized Socrates as a person in his writing, he nevertheless captured for posterity both Socrates' ideas and Plato's own original contributions. In his *Dialogues,* Plato never writes in the first person/in his own voice. In his *Second Letter,* he states "no writing of Plato exists or ever will exist, but those now said to be his are those of a Socrates become beautiful and new." Though some use this to question the *Dialogues'* historical veracity, assuming Plato wrote this statement, it can be seen as simply Plato's way of affirming and deferring to Socrates' original ideas, and also of validating his own ability both to capture and to transform them through his writing. It should be noted that, although many people assume the dialogue form in which Plato wrote represents conversations between the two men, not all scholars believe this is always the reality. Plato may have not only recorded and also interpreted Socrates' ideas; at other times, he may additionally have used the persona of Socrates to express his own thoughts.

In his *Timaeus,* Plato states that the human soul has three parts, located in different parts of the body: Reason, in the head (matching today's information about the brain and thinking); Spirit, in the upper third of the torso (similar to modern characterizations of the "heart"); and Appetite, in the mid-torso down to the navel (corresponding to the physical stomach and small intestine). In his *Dialogues,* Plato quotes Socrates as saying that, like the three-part soul, societies also have three classes or castes. Corresponding to the Appetite is the Productive or Worker class—farmers, ranchers, merchants, carpenters, masons, plumbers, laborers, etc. Corresponding to the Spirit is the Protective, Warrior/Guardian class— soldiers and other strong, brave, adventurous types. Corresponding to the Reason is the Governing, Ruler/Philosopher King class—wise, rational, intelligent, possessing superior self-control and able to govern and make decisions on behalf of their communities. These represented a distinct minority.

Aristotle

Aristotle (384-322 BCE) was born in Macedonia, relocating to Athens, Greece at age 18 to join Plato's Academy until age 37. A polymath, he wrote prolifically on such diverse subjects as biology, zoology, ethics, logic, rhetoric, physics, astronomy, economics, politics, government, linguistics, psychology, theology, aesthetics, metaphysics, theater, poetry music, and more. Only about one-third of his prodigious output remains today. He constructed the first comprehensive philosophical system in the Western world. Following Plato's death, Philip II of Macedon asked Aristotle to tutor his son, Alexander the Great. which he did from 356-323 BCE. This teaching position afforded Aristotle the wherewithal to start a library in his school, the Lyceum, helping him publish many of the hundreds of books he wrote. Although Aristotle subscribed to Platonism during Plato's life, thereafter he refocused to empiricism. He refuted Plato's Theory of Forms that forms—properties, e.g., beauty—existed apart from objects, finding forms intrinsic to objects. Aristotle's belief that all human knowledge and concepts were grounded in perception supported his turn to empiricism. Many of Aristotle's works were founded in his perspectives about the natural sciences, compatible with empirical observation.

Aristotle's work and perspectives regarding the physical sciences not only influenced ancient Greek and Roman thought, but moreover Medieval, Renaissance, Enlightenment, and modern disciplines into the present day. In Rome, Cicero characterized Aristotle's writing style as "a river of gold." In the Middle Ages, Islamic scholars called Aristotle "The First Teacher"; St. Thomas Aquinas called him "The Philosopher." His metaphysical works had deep influences on Jewish, Islamic, and Christian theology and philosophy. The Catholic Church's scholastic tradition was and continues to be influenced by Aristotle. While exceptions were the Enlightenment's classical physics and mechanics pioneered by Isaac Newton in the 18th century, which influenced modern science by providing for both controlled experimentation and foundations in theoretical mathematics, thus representing a departure in methodology, Aristotle's influence was still present in his original concepts that understanding the natural world can be aided by theoretical principles and that everything occurs for some reason. Some observations Aristotle made in zoology were not proven or disproven until the 19th century. His formal study of logic was the first recorded, and was included in modern formal logic later in the 19th century.

In ethics, Aristotle equated the Good with intellectual virtue, based upon reasoning. Rather than a theoretical topic of knowledge for its own sake, Aristotle treated ethics as a practical study whose aim was being and doing good. The *Nicomachean Ethics* was a famous treatise among several he wrote on ethics. Aristotle associated virtue with a thing or being's proper function (*ergon*). Action by the human soul/psyche was a function specific to humans according to reason (*logos*) in Aristotelian ethics. This ideal psychic action was the purpose of all deliberate human activity, i.e., well-being or happiness (*eudaimonia*). Such happiness required moral or ethical virtue or good character. To attain such a virtuous character, Aristotle's teaching was that one must first be conditioned by teachers, and then by experience, toward taking the best actions until one could choose these independently. Living thusly constituted the joint, interdependent development of the intellect (*nous*) and practical thought (*phronesis*) toward attaining the wisdom of a philosopher, i.e., a speculative or theoretical thinker, which Aristotle deemed the highest possible virtue for a human being.

Epicurus

Ancient Greek philosopher Epicurus (c. 342~341-270 BCE) founded Epicureanism, also called the philosophy of the garden because he taught it to his students in the garden of his house in Athens for 36 years until his death. Epicurus, born in the Athenian colony of Samos, studied philosophy from age 14. At 18 he went to Athens, but soon left to escape Perdiccas' rule after Alexander the Great died, joining his father in Colophon; moved to Mitylene, founding a school there; moved to Lampsacus a year later, teaching there for four years; and finally returned to Athens permanently in 306 BCE. Although he produced around 300 written works, nearly all were lost except fragments and several letters summarizing his philosophy, preserved by Diogenes in his *Lives of Eminent Philosophers*, where Diogenes also referred to points Epicurus had made in now lost writings. Some points are also quoted in other authors' works, typically to refute them. Another existing source, *Ta Kuria* (*Sovran Maxims* in English), is a collection of Epicurus' most memorable sayings. Roman authors Lucretius, Cicero, Seneca, and Plutarch also wrote enough about Epicureanism to offer a full knowledge of his philosophy, helping compensate for the loss of Epicurus' own writings.

Democritus, an ancient Greek physicist who was an early atomic theorist, had a strong influence on Epicurus in both his physics and his philosophy. Some scholars find that Epicurus actually formulated his theory of ethics by using Democritean physics as the basis, such that Epicureanism was analogous and complementary to it. Many ancient Greek

- 8 -

philosophers, as well as historians, dramatists, and other intellectuals, frequently resorted to divine intervention to explain the universe, human historical events, and life in general. (Historian and philosopher Thucydides was a notable exception, relying on analyses of human behavior rather than actions by the Greek gods.) Epicurus sought to depart from the tradition of using the gods to explain the universe. Instead, he used analogies with human experience as a way of explaining all events and relationships. By eliminating gods as causal agents, Epicurus found humans were freed to be themselves and hence be happy. Indeed, Epicurus actually defined philosophy as "an activity which by words and arguments secures the happy life."

Epicureanism was divided into the canonic (*to kanonikon* in Greek), the physics (*to phusikon),* and the ethics (*to êthikon*). According to Diogenes in *Lives of Eminent Philosophers,* the canonic introduced Epicurus' philosophical system and took up the entire single book entitled *The Canon.* Diogenes wrote that this includes the standard (*kriterion*), the first principle (*archê*), and the elemental (*stoikeiotikon*). Together these constitute Epicurus' epistemology. The physics covered Epicurus' whole theory of Nature, including birth, growth, and death, which he wrote in 37 books, collectively entitled *Of Nature.* He also summarized these books and his theory of Nature in his letters, which unlike the other works, still exist. The ethics addresses the topics of choice and aversion ("things to be sought and avoided"), and how to live and die. Epicurus wrote about these in his books entitled *On Human Life,* in his letters summarizing his philosophy, and in his treatise entitled *Of the End.*

For Epicurus, feeling was a measure of truth; the two fundamental feelings, pleasure and pain, indicated good and bad. Being based in Nature, these needed no proof. The *telos* or end purpose of all intentional human behavior was pleasure, hence the first or main good; pain is the first or main evil. This defines Epicurean ethics as consequentialist or utilitarian, and eudaemonist (Aristotle's term for happiness or well-being was *eudaimonia*). Epicurus defined pleasure negatively, i.e., not as the presence of pleasant sensations but as the absence of painful sensations and/or psychic disturbances. Further, he distinguished among desires as natural vs. groundless, and natural only vs. natural and necessary. Therefore, he instructed people to avoid acting upon unnatural and unnecessary desires. The goal of a happy life was attained through "health of body" and "tranquility of mind" (*ataraxia*). Epicurus taught that one should pursue only things that removed pain in order to ensure happiness.

Buddhist ethics

The Buddha's enlightened perspective and that of his enlightened followers are the bases for traditional Buddhist ethics. The Buddhist scriptures, and also oral tradition, contain the moral instructions for Buddhists to follow. Hence, to support descriptions of the character of ethics in Buddhism, scholars refer to anthropological findings provided by traditional Buddhist societies, as well as study of the Buddhist scriptures themselves. The Pancasila is a Pali and Sanskrit word meaning the Five Precepts, which are not killing, not stealing, not lying, not engaging in sexual misconduct, and not ingesting intoxicants. For laypeople, taking these five vows constitutes the foundation of Buddhist ethics. However, Buddhist monks and nuns must take several hundred more similar vows, known in Pali and Sanskrit as Vinaya, or discipline. Discipline is one of two main categories of the Buddha's teachings; the other is Dharma, i.e., doctrine. Dharmavinaya, combining both, is a synonym for Buddhism. The Buddhism Middle Way is a more tenable way for Western Buddhists to solve complex modern-world moral problems practically, and can help non-Buddhists understand Buddhist ethics.

An ancient practice of all earlier Buddhas, the Noble Eightfold Path, said to be rediscovered by Gautama Buddha in his search for enlightenment, is a practice to guide disciples to freedom and self-awakening. In some forms of Buddhism it can have three main divisions: concentration, ethical conduct, and wisdom. In Mahayana Buddhism, these are called the Three Higher Trainings: higher concentration, higher ethical conduct, higher wisdom— higher because renunciation (*bodhicitta*) is the motivation to follow in these trainings to attain enlightenment and liberation. This path is the fourth of Buddha's Four Noble Truths, and its first precept, non-injury/non-violence to all living things, explains the four truths. Also called the Middle Way or Middle Path, it is frequently symbolized by the eight-spoked dharma wheel. The path's eight factors are right view and right intention in the wisdom division; right speech, right action, and right livelihood in the ethical conduct division; and right effort, right mindfulness, and right concentration in the concentration division. While many Buddhist ethical precepts are negative or prohibitive, positive virtues include reverence, humility, gratitude, contentment, generosity, patience; political, social, and family duties for societal well-being; and the four underlying "immeasurable" attitudes of compassion, equanimity, loving-kindness, and sympathetic joy.

Hinduism

A belief of the Hindu religion is reincarnation. Therefore, because all beings can live additional lives in other forms, an important Hindu principle is to act for others' benefit selflessly rather than selfishly. Because people can experience desirable or undesirable consequences in the next incarnation from their desirable or undesirable actions in an earlier life, the doctrine of karma yoga applies. In addition, people's individual misfortunes are viewed not only as their own doing but also shared by all people, because individual souls are regarded as sparks of divinity shared among all living beings. Therefore, essential values of Hinduism emphasize hospitality and kindness to others. Empathy is valued more than in many other religious traditions. Hinduism portrays the mother as a divine figure (the Devi), reflected in India's national song of India, which identifies India metaphorically as a Mother; and also treats women at times as gurus and moral models.

Realizing truth through media like visual arts and theater is closely congruent with the Hindu religion: elaborate artwork frequently adorns Hindu temples, and gurus are regarded not only as spiritual guides, but also entertainers. Unusual devotional practices, like conducting pilgrimages over years by rolling on the ground or holding one arm up throughout life, are not only acceptable in Hinduism as valid life choices, but moreover not considered socially deviant or even odd. Historically, the development of caste systems in India, placing people into higher and lower levels of a rigid hierarchy according to birth, exerted influences on Hindu ethical traditions which were unfavorable for those in lower and "untouchable" castes. During the middle of the 20th century, Mohandas Gandhi, whose religion was Vaishnavism, one of the major branches of Hinduism, effected reform of these systems by emphasizing traditions commonly shared by all Indian religions, including nonviolence, harm reduction, and vegetarianism; constructing truth through courage and nonviolent resistance, which he termed *satyagraha;* and rejecting cowardice and concern over physical pain, even injury. Gandhi's work and perspectives have influenced contemporary ethics, particularly in civil rights, social activism, and pacifist and environmental movements.

Jewish ethics

The nexus of ethics as a Western philosophical tradition and Judaism is one way in which Jewish ethics are characterized. They are considered as normative ethics for their goals of addressing a wide variety of moral issues through Judaism's diverse literary works. Another element of Jewish philosophy over 2,000 years has been the dynamics of the interrelationship between ethics and law. The literature of the *halakhah,* i.e., the rabbinical religious legal tradition, has discussed duties not normally punishable by law, its blurred boundaries with these, and many similar ethical issues. The oral Torah interpreted the Old Testament and examined numerous other ethical subjects in early rabbinic Judaism. Later, the written Torah documented Jewish ethics, whose origin is the Old Testament. The Torah (meaning "Teaching") is the first five books (Pentateuch), called in Hebrew and Latin/English respectively, *Bereshit* (In the Beginning), or Genesis; *Shemot* (Names), or Exodus; *Vayikra* (He Called), or Leviticus; *Bamidbar* (In the Desert), or Numbers; and *Devarim* (Things/Words), or Deuteronomy. While the Hebrew (originally Aramaic) Bible includes many other books, the Torah and accompanying commentary of the Talmud are more concerned with Jewish law and ethics.

While rabbinical commentary on Jewish law, ethics, and related topics are found most in the Torah and Talmud, the main themes central to Jewish ethics are also expressed through the books of the Prophets. These themes include the virtues of loving peace, humility, contriteness of spirit, faith, compassion for suffering, kindness to the needy, benevolence, righteousness, and living a righteous life for all individuals. Isaiah advises people to "learn to do good" in order to do away with war and realize an "end-time" of peace and righteous behavior. Jeremiah urges people to fulfill the duty of loyalty to rulers, including foreign ones. A form of the Golden Rule, not to do to others what you find hateful, is stated by the great teacher Hillel in the Talmud; and by 2nd-century Rabbi Akiva, who adds not to hurt, speak ill of, reveal their secrets to others, and hold the honor and property of one's neighbors as dear as one's own, in the Midrash. In addition to loving one's neighbor, Micah emphasizes justice, mercy, humility and walking with God; Isaiah, justice and righteousness; and Habakkuk, righteousness through faithfulness.

Many rabbis have taught justice, truth, and peace (cf. Rabbi Simeon ben Gamaliel) as the most important principles in the world. These values dictate the prohibition of oppression, theft, lying, perjury, swearing falsely, and flattery, as well as revenge and lack of mercy. Judging people according to wealth or poverty is not permitted. The great philosopher, teacher, and author, Rabbi Moshe ben Maimon (Maimonides) wrote that the entire purpose of the Torah was to promote world peace. Simon the Just emphasized Torah, service to God, and especially loving-kindness, closely related to compassion. Self-respect is another Jewish ethical principle, forbidding self-abasement as sinful. Charitable giving is part of the concept of righteousness. Speaking evil, including slander, calumny proper (true but injurious information), and even non-slanderous but mischievous idle talk, is a sin classified together with murder in the Talmud; as are listening to slander or provoking disparaging comments or suspicion. Respect for family and marriage are important. Medical ethics, non-conversion and loving/respecting non-Jews, political governance, care for animals and the environment, and more are also addressed in Jewish ethics.

Christian ethics

Because of the concept of original sin, Christian ethics emphasizes the need to attain forgiveness, mercy, grace, and love. According to the Evangelical counsels, Christians are called to abstain from vice and to make their thoughts and actions increasingly virtuous. Biblical teachings are the foundation of Christian ethical principles. The Christian concept of God's will is based on the Judaic Old Testament Great Commandment to love God with all one's heart, mind, soul, and strength and to love one's neighbor as oneself. The New Testament contributes the concept of loving one's enemy or turning the other cheek. The concept of grace, the basis of Christian ethics, enables people to make righteous choices and actions and transforms their lives. Both sin and grace are concepts applicable to both individuals and societies. The Old Testament Book of Isaiah's vision of the righteous society living in harmony and peace with nature and God, i.e., the Kingdom of God, imparts a teleological element (the idea of definite finality in nature) to Christian ethics.

The reason for common references to the Judeo-Christian tradition is that the two are so similar: Jesus Christ was a Jew, so his teachings were based in Judaic ethics; his followers were called Christians. The Old Testament's First Commandment is the same in both religions, to love God above all and love neighbors as oneself. One major difference from Jewish ethics found in Christian ethics is also to love one's enemies. Some theologians (e.g., Meyer, Yoder) believe Jesus' teachings to go the second mile, turn the other cheek, etc. were products of a non-violent protest Jesus staged against Roman enemies. Viewing teachings to eschew violence, not retaliate, and love one's opponents as components of a larger campaign for nonviolence requires interpreting Christian ethics as social, not only individual; and focused on earthly life. Additional principles include eschewing hypocrisy, materialism, power, and wealth; preserving personal integrity, honesty, and loyalty; and teaching others through Godly devotion, personal happiness, and joy. In addition to the Seven Virtues and Seven Deadly Sins, St. Paul cited virtues of faith, hope and charity in Corinthians; St. Thomas Aquinas added Aristotle's four cardinal virtues: justice, courage, temperance, and prudence.

Confucianism

In the Chinese Confucian religion, ethics focus on the importance of maintaining relationships and their propriety. Doing what one's relationships need is considered ethical. Obligations toward other people are determined by proximity or distance; i.e., individuals owe nothing to strangers, but everything to their parents. In acknowledging that one cannot love everybody in the world simultaneously and equally, Confucianism ethics are considered situational ethics or relational ethics. However, this differs from Kant's situational ethics by seldom including universal or absolute principles or laws. Regarding leadership, Confucius said the ideal ruler "acts like the North Star, staying in place while the other stars orbit around it." This means that rulers should produce harmony, not laws; and lead by example, not try to force good behavior in their subjects. Because of this, many scholars have characterized Chairman Mao Zedong as more Confucian than Communist in his leadership.

One principle that Confucius found of paramount value above all others was that of honesty. He found this so important that, in establishing a code of traditional practices, Confucius actually effected fundamental semantic changes to the previous conceptual meanings of certain Chinese vocabulary words related to honesty. For example, he formulated concepts for the Chinese words *lǐ, yì,* and *rén* to signify more profound demonstrations of honesty; *pinyin: chéng,* translated literally as "sincerity"; and *pinyin: xiào,* translated as "fidelity." These concepts indicated honest, sincere, and faithful behavior toward one's parents, to whom one owed one's existence; and toward one's colleagues, neighbors, and inferiors in rank, to whom one owed one's survival. The influence of Mahayana Buddhism's metaphysic added cohesion and a more universalist emphasis to Chinese philosophy.

In a reaction against the domination of Buddhism during the Tang Dynasty, Neo-Confucianism developed as an effort to establish a native Confucian analytical and metaphysical structure. The Confucian model of the ruler and family held continued predominance in Chinese society and life until the beginning of the 20th century. By then, the hierarchies of inflexible property rights legislated under Imperial regimes had ultimately changed the traditional Confucian ethics into a legalized system characteristic of dictatorships in general. One principle that Confucianism and Taoism share in common is their belief in the essential goodness of human nature. However, while the primary Confucian branch maintains that culture, ritual, and other societal products and practices should be used to nurture human nature, Taoism, in contrast, maintains that the better way to affirm the goodness of human nature is to do away with the accoutrements of society. Whereas Confucius said that ideal rulers should lead by example rather than by action, Laozi and other Taoist philosophers extended this passivity further, to virtual inactivity.

Islamic ethics

Reflection about the meaning of life, which is believed to indicate the existence of God, is one of the foundations of Islamic ethics. The concept that humanity has been given the ability to identify God's will and to adhere to it is also basic to the development and codification of Muslim ethics. Islam finds that humans are morally responsible to abide by God's will and follow the rules of Islam as stated in the teachings of Muhammad, the Qur'an, and the Sunnah. The human attachment to materialism is represented in the Qur'an as subversive to humankind's natural tendency to follow the divine will. While this begins as basic survival and security needs, it evolves into a need to stand out in society. Islamic scriptures find this materialistic tendency causes ignorance (*jahilyya*) and interferes with people's intrinsic reflective abilities. Muhammad is regarded as dispatched by God, like other Muslim prophets, to remind humans of their moral responsibility and oppose societal ideas that would subvert submitting to God.

Islamic tradition has sought to eliminate: (1) multiple tribal divisions according to blood relations and kinship, which Islam would replace with an *ummah* or unified community founded on Islamic piety. (2) Polytheism, the belief in multiple gods, which monotheistic Islam would replace with Allah alone. (3) *Muruwwa* ("manliness"), an Arabic equivalent of the Spanish term *machismo*; Islam discouraged this, preferring piety and humility instead. (4) Desires to attain fame and/or create legacies. Islam would replace this with the idea that on the day of resurrection, all humankind would be accountable to God. (5) Ancestral traditions, which Arab peoples followed and revered. Islam would challenge these by placing priority on the submission to God and the following of revelation instead. These shifts in values reoriented and ultimately transformed Arabian Peninsula moral structure and society. Muslim ethical values also advocate humility, both with God and other people; and maintaining control over one's desires and passions. They eschew arrogance, insolence, vanity, and materialism.

According to the Qur'an and the teachings of the prophet Muhammad, money, jobs, and possessions are viewed as tools for becoming better people, not as end goals in themselves. In Islamic ethics, people are to be pious and humble not only with God, but also with other people. They are expected not only to avoid evil or sinful acts themselves, but moreover to forbid others to engage in these. They are expected not only to be virtuous themselves, but also to get others to behave virtuously. Therefore, Muslims are expected not only to be morally healthy themselves, but furthermore to contribute to ensuring the entire society's moral health. Mohammad described just speech, regardless of emotion; moderation, regardless of income; reuniting with friends who have broken off with one; giving to those who refuse one; and requiring what is right as qualities he included in a summary of ideal Muslim conduct.

Epictetus and stoicism

Epictetus was born into slavery around 55 AD, presumed in Hierapolis, Phrygia (Pamukkale, Turkey today). His given name was unknown. *Epíktetos* means "acquired" in Greek. He grew up in Rome as a slave to rich Roman Epaphroditos, Emperor Nero's secretary, who permitted Epictetus to pursue his interest in philosophy. Epictetus studied Stoic philosophy with Musonius Rufus. This education gained him respectability. Artwork shows him with a crutch. Accounts of his disability vary: Simplicius wrote his lameness dated from childhood, while Origen wrote his master had purposely broken Epictetus' leg. After Nero died in 68 AD, Epictetus attained freedom, teaching philosophy in Rome until c. 93 AD, when Emperor Domitian exiled all philosophers. Epictetus then lived in Epirus, Greece, founding a philosophy school there. His student, Arrian, credited the content of his famed *Discourses* to Epictetus's lectures, characterizing Epictetus as a powerful orator who skillfully influenced audience emotions. Emperor Hadrian and many other prominent Greeks befriended and conversed with Epictetus. He lived simply with few material things, never marrying. In old age, he rescued a child from death, adopting and raising him with a woman's help. He died c.135 AD.

The ancient Greek philosophy of Stoicism is the origin of our contemporary term "stoic," meaning the quality of enduring difficulties without showing emotion. This stems from the original Stoic philosophy that wisdom included acceptance of whatever life events transpired. Stoicism taught that people should control their emotions and reactions. Socrates' own brave and calm acceptance of his death, which he could have escaped had he chosen, influenced the Stoics' and Epictetus' approaches. Epictetus maintained a constantly positive attitude in spite of his physical disability. He taught that all humans have the potential for happiness and virtue, which they could realize through consistent self-control and character. Epictetus defined self-control in two respects—controlling one's senses, and controlling one's attitude regarding reality. He wrote, "I cannot escape death, but I can escape the dread of it." This ancient philosophy is the origin of today's psychological counsel that, though we cannot control events, we can control how we react to them. Epictetus believed that we can even control fear through exerting our will.

Stoicism is called practical because it espouses an approach to life that is, above all, realistic. Epictetus wrote that what upset people were "not things... but rather ideas about things." Using Socrates' acceptance of death as an example, he wrote that death itself was not terrible, but rather "the idea that death is terrible that is terrible." He advocated not blaming others but our own ideas for our feeling upset, grief, or frustration. He considered blaming others for one's problems "philosophically ignorant." Moreover, he believed that, whereas people blaming themselves were "beginning to learn," the "educated person" blamed "neither anyone else nor himself." Another realistic aspect of Epictetus' philosophy found in many contemporary philosophical and psychological disciplines is the idea that, to be happy, we should embrace what is rather than wishing it were different: He wrote, 'Don't seek for things to happen as you wish, but wish for things to happen as they do, and you will get on well."

"Apathy" in Stoic terms, differing from contemporary meanings of lacking motivation or interest, means self-control to free us from jealousies and desires, equated with wisdom bringing happiness and serenity. Stoicism uses the metaphor of an actor with a smaller role in a play: rather than being jealous or resentful of the star and/or wishing to no avail to be the storyteller, every individual does not choose his/her "role" in life, but is assigned it by the play's writer/director, i.e., by God in real life. Stoics deemed it wisdom to acknowledge and accept one's role in life's drama. Epictetus taught we should "habituate" ourselves by forbearing with abuse, enduring labor, and controlling ourselves against temptation, so as not to "be carried away by impressions." This reflects the Platonic distinction between life's appearances as transitory and illusory, vs. the Ideal as eternal and real. Epictetus also wrote that overindulgence in appetites—gustatory, alcoholic, excretory, or sexual—was "the sign of a weak mind." He believed bodily needs should be satisfied "incidentally" with more attention focused on the mind.

St. Thomas Aquinas

In his moral philosophy, Aquinas (1225-1274) combined the Greek Aristotle's concept of happiness or *eudaimonia* with Christianity's theology. He believed in Aristotelian teleology as determining goodness or badness of actions insofar as they promoted or prevented the *telos* or ultimate purpose of humanity, and in moral and intellectual virtues as informing and motivating human pursuit and attainment of happiness. He also believed in the Christian tradition of deification—i.e., God's transformative perfecting of human nature—as a requirement, beyond the virtues, for divine beatitude—i.e., uniting with God—as the only true or complete happiness; and in our need for this to overcome Adam and Eve's original sin and hence our inherited tendency toward sinning. Aquinas believed that, due to this taint of sin, human will was at cross purposes with God's will. Therefore, he taught that God's grace, which endows humans with gifts and virtues of divine origin, was necessary to return complete good to human nature, to make it congruent with the divine will.

In his *Confessions,* St. Augustine stated that existence itself conferred some inherent goodness to things while finding some things incorruptible, others corruptible. Corruptible things could lose goodness, necessarily having goodness to lose. Augustine concluded things with no goodness at all must not exist. In his *Summa Theologicae,* Aquinas reflected this idea, equating goodness with being; and rejected the reality of evil per se. He wrote something was evil if "deprived of some particular good that pertains to its due or proper perfection"—showing his belief in Aristotle's teleological concept of good or evil as realizing or inhibiting humanity's ultimate goal or *telos*. Aquinas' idea of evil agreed with Augustine's: existence bestowed good, nothing existing was totally devoid of goodness, and things containing some evil had somehow had their existence corrupted. Aristotle's study of natural life also influenced Aquinas, in Aristotle's idea that the organizing Form of a thing/being was its nature. Aquinas extended this conception, saying all substances seek to realize their existence fully through perfection, both realizing their goodness and actually comprising their good. Contemporary humanistic psychologist Abraham Maslow's "self-actualization," i.e., humans' seeking to realize their full potential, is another permutation of these ideas.

(1) Prudence: Aquinas called prudence wisdom or reason regarding moral judgments and decisions, requiring understanding of both universal rational principles and specific decision-making circumstances. This required the ability to evaluate individual, complex situations rather than simply applying moral principles uniformly. Prudence illuminated the best course of action to attain the human good, our predetermined goal, Aristotle's *telos*. (2) Temperance: Aquinas defined temperance as both general moral and specific appetitive moderation. Again the influence of Aristotle, who advocated "moderation to all things," is present. Aquinas found moderation granted more lasting and satisfying pleasure than immoderate self-indulgence. His concept of temperance included humility, studiousness, clemency, and restraining idle curiosity and punitive and angry urges. (3) Courage: while he did not see fear as inherently opposing reason, Aquinas' virtue of courage moderated fear, to keep it both from inhibiting necessary actions and from acting recklessly and dangerously. Courage included endurance, confidence, and perseverance. (4) Justice: Aquinas saw (a) legal/general or particular and (b) commutative and distributive justice as guiding human relationships and citizenship and governing the other virtues.

Thomas Hobbes

Scholars find the influence of British 17th-century philosopher Hobbes stronger in political philosophy than moral philosophy, attributing this to his political philosophy's being more definitive contrasted with the ambiguity of his moral philosophy. While his political works include *The Elements of Law, Natural and Politic* (1650); *Philosophical Rudiments Concerning Government and Society* (1651); *De Corpore* (1655); *The Questions Concerning Liberty, Necessity, and Chance* (1656); *De Homine* (1658); *Behemoth* (1679); and *Dialogue Between a Philosopher and a Student of the Common Laws of England* (1681); it is *Leviathan* (1651 in English, 1668 in Latin) that is considered his masterpiece. Interpretations of his moral philosophy vary because he believed "the true Morall philosophie" consisted of "the true doctrine of the Lawes of Nature," and interpretations of what he wrote about the laws of nature also vary. Having experienced the political deterioration leading to the English Civil War, Hobbes searched for rational principles to establish governmental stability. He believed obedience to absolute political authority was the only alternative to the inherent self-destruction from within of other forms of government through civil war.

Scholars today view Hobbes as having attained equal stature with Plato, Aristotle, Locke, Rousseau, Kant, and Rawls in the realm of political philosophy, particularly for *Leviathan*. Predating Locke, he extensively developed the theory of the social contract. However, whereas Locke later emphasized in his *Second Treatise of Government* the power of the social contract to preserve individual rights and maintained that the state of nature was preferable to being ruled by a monarch with absolute power, Hobbes had the opposite view: he applied the concept of the social contract to conclude that submission to an absolute governing authority was necessary to maintain security and prevent the dissolution of civilized society. He wrote that "masterlesse men, without subjection to Lawes, and a coercive Power to tye their hands" [from evil acts] would preclude the development of culture, industry, machinery, navigation, importation, building, geography, history, literature, or the arts, and would promote humanity's constant danger and fear of "violent death."

When Hobbes wrote in *Leviathan* that, without the security and stability that only the rule of an absolute government could provide, he described such a "dissolute condition" famously as "the life of man, solitary, poore, nasty, brutish, and short." He equated the state of nature with the state of war, writing that if "a man is in the condition of mere nature, (which is a condition of war,) as private appetite is the measure of good and evil." He found people could only avoid such a miserable state of nature by collectively acknowledging and obeying an absolute political authority. Hence many find his characterization of the state of nature as overly pessimistic. However, scholars find it plausible through multiple normative and empirical assumptions he established: Hobbes' assumption of people's physical and mental similarities dictates none can dominate others or be invulnerable. His assumption that people fear death supports the power of human self-preservation instincts, which he terms "the right of nature." His assumptions of human bias, limited altruism, vulnerability to insults based on inflated self-images, and objectifying subjective preferences as "good/bad" have ample evidence. He attributes religious beliefs to human curiosity about causality and anxiety about the future.

John Locke

Locke believed we learn moral concepts of good and evil informing moral law, and are motivated to follow moral rules through his idea of Hedonism in his moral theory, supporting his moral legalism: Locke believed laws must threaten sanctions to function normatively. Generally, pleasure and pain were primary motivators for all human thought and behavior. Morally, good and evil were reducible to these: things were good or evil depending whether they evoked pleasure or pain. He did not distinguish moral from natural good and evil qualitatively, but contextually, e.g., physical pleasure is evoked by smelling a rose, moral good equals the pleasure of complying with moral rules, and moral evil equals pain from violating them. Locke characterized reward and punishment as specific, legal pleasure and pain. For him, the extent to which legislative authorities could impose sanctions on citizens determined their power over them. Locke's ultimate superior with authority to enforce rewards and punishment was God. His ethics of belief found human reason divinely provided the potential to understand morality, but often failing. He viewed sanctions as assuring the law of moral rules for "those who refuse to be led by reason," reflecting Hobbes' belief in submission to authority.

John Locke's *An Essay Concerning Human Understanding*
Although in this Essay, Locke does not develop his concept of morality as fully as many other ideas he wrote about, the work is nonetheless considered not only motivated primarily by his considerations of morality, but moreover a definitive representation of 17th-century metaphysics and empirical epistemology. Many scholars have avoided critically analyzing this work, intimidated by their impression that it is too complex, even incomprehensible. Some also find his essay's marked rationalism contradictory to Locke's reputation as his time's preeminent empiricist. However, Locke regarded morality, like mathematics, as differing from other subjects by enabling human thought to reach any degree of rational certainty. He saw our reasoning as deficient with respect to understanding nature and human psychology, but much better equipped for determining the moral duties of humankind. Moreover, the moral philosophy described by Locke reflects the 17th century's theory of natural law, and most likely its prevailing moral perspective.

In *Essays on the Law of Nature,* Locke emphasized reason as how we understand moral laws, including how we appreciate morality's divine, hence righteous nature; and how we understand morality as legal authority's expression. He wrote that moral laws were best understood with reference to legal authority to distinguish them from social conventions. He equated human law with natural law in meeting three requirements: (1) being based on a superior's will, (2) functioning to set behavioral rules, and (3) binding people with duty to comply with the superior lawmaking authority. Locke's early writings reflect Aristotle's and Aquinas' teleology: "the proper function of man is acting in conformity with reason." He found moral duty obligatory, specifically reflective of human nature, and fulfilling divine will. Though he rejected teleology in favor of empiricism in *An Essay Concerning Human Understanding,* Locke used teleological elements in his moral theory to support a theological foundation for natural law. In *Essays on the Law of Nature,* he in turn used his empiricist epistemology as the basis for developing his moral rationalism. He saw moral rules as based on principles similar to mathematical axioms that we can rationally deduce, and thence deduce our moral obligations.

Jean-Jacques Rousseau

Rousseau (1712-1778), born in Switzerland, relocating to France in adulthood and then returning to Geneva, made contributions to music, religion, moral psychology, human social development, literature, linguistics, botany, and Diderot's and d'Alembert's *Encyclopédie.* In his 1750 *First Discourse [on the Sciences and Arts],* Rousseau argued that social, artistic, and scientific development motivated by desires for individual excellence and distinction degraded individual moral character and civic virtue, winning him an award and fame. He developed his themes from this work on the common person's natural virtue and the moral corruption caused by desires to excel individually in later works, including his 1755 *Second Discourse [on the Origins of Inequality].* His successful 1761 epistolary novel *Julie, ou La Nouvelle Héloïse;* his 1762 book *Emile,* which profoundly influenced psychology and education as well as philosophy; and his 1762 book *The Social Contract* were deemed heretical in both France and Switzerland, forcing Rousseau to England, where he was invited by British philosopher David Hume. Rousseau influenced French Enlightenment thought and developed theories of human social development and moral psychology.

Rousseau asserted his worldview revolved around believing humans were by nature good, but corrupted by society. He named the human instinct for self-preservation "self-love" (*amour de soi*), which he found God-given for meeting our natural, basic needs. He also identified compassion (*pitié*), whereby humans address suffering in animals and other humans when this does not endanger their own survival. In some works, Rousseau portrayed *pitié* as distinct from self-love; in others, as an outgrowth of self-love which he characterized as the source of all passions. In *Discourse on the Origins of Inequality,* Rousseau envisioned human evolution whereby people successively alter their physical and mental interactions and hence self-conceptions. He found humans distinct from other beings only through freedom and perfectibility, which enabled developing self-consciousness, rationality, and morality but could conversely create deceptive, oppressed, dependent societies. Rousseau viewed the shift from nomadic hunter-gatherer to settled farming communities as a central transition, triggering a shift from self-love to sexual/social competition, *amour propre,* which encompassed both humankind's failure, and its redemption through developing human rationality and social and educational organization.

Rousseau's most complete discussions of morality are in his *Lettres Morales* and in parts of the section of *Emile* entitled *Confessions of Faith of the Savoyard Vicar.* Rousseau saw *pitié* (compassion) as countering self-love (*amour de soi*) during primitive human life before *amour propre* (sexual/social competition) developed, but found this more instinctive than genuine morality, which he felt required applying reason to human behavior and relations and involving conscience, which motivated love for morality and justice. He saw conscience as people's rationally appreciating God's well-ordered world plan. But he felt that, more often in society, human reason was used for oppression, exploitation, and domination than for sympathy. In Rousseau's *Second Discourse* and *Letter to d'Alembert,* he includes the theme of human self-deception regarding their own morality. As an example, theatrical tragedies could evoke audience compassion; but then, feeling naturally good, audiences felt license for vicious behaviors outside of the play. Rousseau also commented in *The State of War* that philosophy could enable people to rationalize laws denying natural *pitié* and allowing violence and oppression.

Thomas Jefferson

According to Jefferson, a nation is based upon a moral foundation which determines the relationships among its individual citizens, the collective national character, the character of the government with which those people choose to live, and is an integral component of how those people interact. Jefferson saw true morality as a development of human nature and human life, the same as he saw our natural, inalienable rights. Thus he found it impossible to think about any political philosophy adequately or intelligently without including its moral aspects as a part of it. He felt the love of other people and the sense of duty to them, which he called "a moral instinct," were endowed to humans by God and nature. Jefferson reasoned that God meant humans to be social animals by placing them in social contexts. A government based on individual freedom would allow citizens to live with security and interact in mutually beneficial ways, meaning that a moral opportunity is inherent in liberty. He wrote (1789): "Liberty... is the great parent of science and... virtue;... a nation will be great in both always in proportion as it is free."

Jefferson believed the thoughts and feelings of reasonable, good people supplied ample evidence of moral law. He wrote (1793), "the head and heart of every rational and honest man" were where "nature has written her moral laws, and where every man may read them for himself." While moral rules founded only on rationalism could be manipulated to justify all sorts of actions, frequently according to individual biases and wants for importance, superiority, and/or group membership instead of natural human sensibilities or social justice requirements, Jefferson found natural human sentiments would combat such intellectual distortions, usually prevailing eventually in most people. He wrote (1809), "The practice of morality being necessary for the well-being of society, [our Creator] has taken care to impress its precepts so indelibly on our hearts... they shall not be effaced by the subtleties of our brain." Jefferson believed the same principles ruled personal/individual and national/social morality; and that individual, national and international relations harmonized with natural human rights. He believed loving/helping others must be morally informed by respect, responsibility for promoting mutual happiness, and the principle of equal burdens and benefits as necessary parts of a just society.

Jefferson identified these essential components of social, moral interaction: dealing honestly with all, acting benevolently toward "those who fall within our way," respecting others' rights, and cherishing others' freedom of conscience. Honesty: He wrote, "Truth is... a branch of morality... very important... to society." He believed that "Men are disposed to live honestly, if the means... are open to them." He stated, "Good faith ought... to be the rule of action in public as well as... private transactions." Acting benevolently: Jefferson saw it as our duty to give what we could spare to the needy, including ensuring distribution appropriate to need and doing so personally rather than through agents and to persons "whom we know not" in countries "from which we get no account." Respecting rights: Jefferson described respecting others' equal rights as defining liberty and morality. Cherishing freedom of conscience: Jefferson identified this right as that of one who is truly free to form opinions, make decisions about issues, and act on those decisions without violating others' rights as being essential to personal liberty.

Immanuel Kant

Kant (1724-1804) proposed what he named the Categorical Imperative (CI) as a standard of rationalism, the basis for moral dictates. Immorality involved violating the CI, thus making it irrational. Although Hobbes and Locke had also based moral laws on rational standards before Kant, theirs were either intuitive or instrumental principles. While Kant agreed with them and others that analyzing practical rationality would only show that rational agency had to adhere to instrumental principles, he nonetheless maintained that the non-instrumental principle of adhering to the CI and thus to moral rules could be proven necessary to rational agents. The foundation of this proposal was Kant's belief that a rational will was free in that it authored the law governing it, i.e., it was autonomous. The CI, the foundational principle of morality, equals a free/autonomous will's law. Kant believed that every individual's possession of this self-regulating rationality justified regarding every individual as equally deserving and worthy of equal respect.

The most influential arguments of Kant are in his *The Groundwork of the Metaphysics of Morals, The Critique of Practical Reason, The Metaphysics of Morals, Anthropology from a Pragmatic Point of View,* and *Religion within the Boundaries of Mere Reason.* In the first-named of these works, Kant devotes the first two chapters to the most fundamental aim of moral philosophy, which he writes is to identify ("seek out") the founding principle of any moral metaphysics. He then analyzes and explains common moral notions in an effort to state specifically which principle(s) is/are the basis of all everyday human moral judgments. Today, Kant's views on the degree and depth of moral accord may often be thought too optimistic. However, he did identify a moral perspective very generally, widely, and deeply shared. Kant's second fundamental aim is to establish a basic moral principle as deriving from every individual's rational will, based on the assumption that people with rational wills have autonomy.

In addition to these two aims, Kant also found moral philosophy should account for the quality and degree of different ethical duties based on fundamental moral principles. In his *The* Groundwork *of the Metaphysics of Morals,* Kant classified people's main ethical duties to self and others. He additionally found moral philosophy must describe and explain what morality requires of human psychological and social character and interaction. He discussed this subject in his second *Critique, The Metaphysics of Morals,* and extensively in *Anthropology from a Pragmatic Point of View.* Kant felt these aims of moral philosophy were indicated to answer, "What ought I to do?" Religious and political needs must also be considered to answer this fully, constituting indirect ethical duties to Kant which he discussed in *Religion* and *The Metaphysics of Morals.* Another aim of moral philosophy Kant saw was addressing the Highest Good—humanity's ultimate goal, Aristotle's *telos*—and its relation to morality. Total happiness plus total moral virtue represented Kant's Highest Good. Virtue enabled deserving, though not guaranteeing or necessarily even facilitating, happiness. Yet Kant believed reason demanded immortality/eternity and divinely assured well-being as "postulates" concerning moral subjects.

Jeremy Bentham

Bentham (1748-1832) took influences from the psychological egoism of Thomas Hobbes's description of human nature, and David Hume's doctrine of the social utility of the artificial virtues. Harking back to the Hedonism and consequentialism of Epicurus and other ancient Greek philosophers as well as their contemporary reflections, Bentham also believed seeking pleasure and avoiding pain were the ruling human drives. But he additionally agreed with the concept of utility being the standard of correct individual and governmental behavior. Bentham found that bad laws caused unhappiness without any balancing happiness, making them lack utility: a law or action that did no good was no good. This informed his interest in legal and social reform. Utilitarianism, like egoism, believes that actions that do the most good are morally best. The scope of the pertinent consequences of actions is the distinction between egoism and utilitarianism: egoism considers the good of the self, whereas utilitarianism also considers the overall good of others. This overall good is also impartial: both promoting it and reaping its benefits are identical, not individual.

Although Bentham acknowledged Hobbes's influence, a major difference between the two is that Hobbes advised moral actions promoting the overall good only if they were congruent with one's own individual welfare. Applying this principle interferes with understanding Bentham's moral philosophy because Bentham also subscribed to Hume's idea of the social utility of moral actions in promoting the overall social good. At times Bentham appeared to attempt to reconcile this contradiction between self-interest and societal well-being empirically by equating action promoting the overall good with also benefiting the individual self. However, Bentham specified the extent of pleasure/good as a criterion in his method for moral decision-making, which discouraged focusing on self-interest. His awareness of this contradiction contributed to his not committing wholeheartedly to ethical egoism in his later career, when he conceded people would at times behave to benefit overall humanity's good. While influenced by Hume in viewing utility as indicating virtue, Bentham tended more toward evaluation of action than Hume's evaluation of character. This was consistent with Bentham's concern for social and legal reform: actions are more accessible and relevant than character in legislation.

The form of Hedonism espoused by Bentham was both optimistic and straightforward. As an example of his optimism, he believed pain could be mitigated, relieved, or changed if it could be proven to be founded on false beliefs. As an example of straightforwardness, he did not believe such pain based on false beliefs should be ignored. Bentham observed that people would often represent their physical dislike of some social or behavioral practice as a moral prohibition, and then use this pretense to justify punishing individuals who engaged in acts they found offensive. Bentham found this invalid on several levels. For one, he pointed out that using prejudice or poor taste as grounds for punishment would produce endless punishments, as "one should never know where to stop." He found that demonstrating prejudice was "ill-grounded" would address it. Regarding the principles of pleasure/goodness and pain/badness for moral decision-making, Bentham applied these criteria: the pleasure or pain's intensity; duration; certainty (how likely it results from the concerned action); proximity (immediacy of pain/pleasure to the action); fecundity (likelihood of producing additional pain/pleasure); purity (how much pain and pleasure are mixed); and extent, i.e., how many people the action affects.

Bentham articulated a number of criteria for evaluating moral decisions, i.e., the intensity, duration, certainty, proximity, fecundity, purity, and extent of the pleasure and/or pain produced by an action. However, he also realized the time-consuming and complex nature of keeping track of all these rules. He did not advise using them to inform every moral decision as this would be inefficient. Instead, he advocated that people use experience as their guide. For example, we might derive pleasure from kicking some people under some circumstances, but the pain this would inflict would usually outweigh our pleasure. This simple equation obviates the need for complicated moral deliberations. Consensus, previous experiences, and rules of thumb can apply as guidance to many actions. Yet Bentham noted people could override these guidelines when they would compromise promoting overall good. His views were unusual to many contemporaries in that he determined actions' moral quality instrumentally, not by inherent right or wrong. While Bentham valued liberty and autonomy, he saw them not as intrinsically good, but as instrumentally good. Actions violating liberty or autonomy were bad instrumentally, not inherently. This deviated markedly from Enlightenment philosophers' invocation of natural law, and Kant's orientation to moral evaluation.

Bentham viewed morally good and bad decisions not as natural or unnatural or intrinsically good and bad, but only as instrumentally good and bad, i.e., in terms of their consequences. It then logically followed that his political philosophy and approach to social policy were informed by this instrumentalist approach. Bentham saw the law not as an immutable concept set in stone, but as a live, changing, evolving process. Because the consequences of any policy could change at any time under different circumstances, that policy's moral quality could also change as a result. He felt the continually changing character of lawmaking as it responded and adjusted to people's various and shifting wants must be acknowledged (cf. Rosenblum, 1978). Therefore, Bentham found legislators must be aware of and sensitive to changes in social conditions and events. Critics of this position maintain certain actions are inherently wrong morally, no matter their consequences, and therefore, certain laws reflect and regulate such actions. The more challenging burden of proof that consequences are the sole criteria for morally evaluating policies and actions would fall to Bentham in defending his position.

Adam Smith

In *Theory of Moral Sentiments* (1759), Adam Smith established a distinctive and comprehensive form of moral sentimentalism. Taking this work together with his famous economics work *The Wealth of Nations,* readers can infer his political perspectives as well, though he did not state these as overtly. A major theme throughout Smith's writing is a markedly strong devotion to the ordinary person's soundness of judgment, accompanied by a corresponding rejection of policymakers' and philosophers' efforts to substitute systems designed by intellectuals that they presumed superior. In "History of Astronomy," Smith portrays philosophy as concerned with regularizing and connecting data of people's everyday experiences. In *Theory of Moral Sentiments,* he begins with ordinary moral judgments as bases for developing moral theory instead of with a higher philosophical perspective. In *The Wealth of Nations,* he opposes the idea that government authorities must guide ordinary citizens' economic decisions. Similarly to David Hume's rejection of philosophy's ability to replace commonplace life judgments, Smith suspected foundationalist philosophical perspectives outside of the practices and thinking they analyze.

Adam Smith did not trust philosophy when it approached the lives of everyday individuals from a foundationalist point of view, i.e., from without and above those lives. Rather, he traced everyday life from the inside. Neither criticizing nor justifying ordinary life from an external perspective, Smith instead chose to use his own methods and tools to correct any flaws he saw in common life from within. Smith's purpose was to dismantle and ultimately do away with the differentiation between theoretical thought and ordinary thinking. His interest in doing this was related to and influenced by his political interests, namely his desire to guarantee ordinary people the "natural liberty" to make decisions and take actions—economically, politically, and otherwise—that were done according to their own judgments, not those of others including philosophers, other intellectuals, or governmental authorities. Natural rights, given to people by God and/or Nature, were a prominent theme of moral and political philosophy during Enlightenment of the 17th and 18th centuries, reflected in Smith's works as well as those of Locke, Rousseau, Kant, and many others, and continued in contemporary ethical philosophies, e.g., that of Nozick.

Smith opens his *Theory of Moral Sentiments* with a discussion of sympathy. He finds the origin of sympathy to be our speculating how we would feel if experiencing what others did. In contrast to David Hume's version of sympathy, which is actually more like empathy—feeling what other people feel in the same situations, or as some put it, "contagion" sympathy—Smith describes sympathy more projectively. This allows potential for our feelings on someone else's behalf to differ from theirs. Because imagining a situation is naturally less intense than experiencing it firsthand, sympathizers' emotions are never identical to original experiencers', which Smith found very significant. He strongly emphasized the primary human drive of observers for closely sharing feelings of other people—agents and objects alike—and adjusting our emotions sympathetically, generating virtues including emotional self-control, humanity, and compassion through striving to participate in others' experiences. Smith equated sympathizing as he believed an impartial observer would to morally approving others' feelings. Moral ideals and norms, and our judgments toward them, emerged from the reciprocal sympathy process.

Smith differentially identified moral rules and virtues as behavioral norms. Moral rules emerged from human reactions against specific examples of behaviors like murder, rape, or stealing. These reactions supplied society with common behavioral expectations not to do such things. Society cannot exist without justice, to which moral rules are necessary. In addition, moral rules help people see through the common biased human misperceptions, which Smith called our "veil of self-delusion." They also support the many people with marginal virtue to ensure a modicum of decent behavior and decorum. Smith found virtue needed not just following moral rules alone, but moreover adopting an impartial observer's sentiments by identifying with them rather than only affecting them. He felt that being virtuous involved not only obeying moral rules, but within those parameters, functioning independently of rules by endeavoring skillfully to shape our emotional dispositions to develop appropriate endurance, patience, courage, kindness, and gratitude.

The ethics Smith describes in his *Theory of Moral Sentiments* has more in common with virtue ethics than with Kant and the Utilitarian school's moral systems governed primarily by rules. However, he also includes these other ethical concepts of compliance with general moral rules. Scholars find his ideas on the need for rules to avert self-deception from depending only on sentiment as precursors to Kant's criticism of moral sentimentalism. Regarding consequentialism, Smith agrees we judge actions by consequences as well as intentions, finding this appropriate providing we consider intended, not just actual, consequences. He differentiates actions' propriety from their consequences as two separate components of moral judgment, deeming the former more important than the latter. However, he concedes that, in certain instances, consequences can assume primary importance, as when endangering society's survival. In the last edition of *Theory of Moral Sentiments,* Smith added Part VI, introducing character portraits illustrating virtues of self-control, prudence, and benevolence; and Part VII, emphasizing Plato, Aristotle, and the Stoics' contributions in a brief history of moral philosophy, indicating his preference for character virtues above decision-making procedures. Smith appeared to hope ancient Greek ethics would be revived, with contemporary revisions.

John Stuart Mill

Mill (1806-1873) followed, admired, and was influenced by Jeremy Bentham. However, he differed with Bentham in some areas, especially regarding the nature of happiness. Bentham maintained that pleasure varied quantitatively (in extent, intensity, duration, etc.), but not qualitatively. Simple and sensual pleasures to Bentham were equal to more complex and sophisticated ones. Critics found this an overly egalitarian approach to Hedonism. Bentham's negation of qualitatively different pleasures was criticized on the grounds that this made human and animal pleasures equal, hence equating their moral value and the moral status of harming either one. Mill wanted to revise Bentham's theory to address these criticisms. (Today, humane advocates endeavoring to overcome assumptions of lower moral status/value accompanying the mistreatment of animals would likely side more with Bentham than Mill.) To make Bentham's Hedonism more specific, Mill applied "perfectionist" influences, assigning relatively greater/lesser values to various pleasures. Though in this sense, Mill's perception of the good departed drastically from Bentham's, they both equated good with the psychological state of pleasure. Their theories were structurally similar. Though Mill accepted concepts of rights more than Bentham, he nevertheless accepted Utilitarianism, applying utilitarian rationales for all rights he identified.

Mill, unlike Bentham, maintained that some pleasures, e.g., intellectual ones, were superior in quality to other pleasures. He did not defend this by appealing to intuition, but by referring to experience: he stated that people who experienced both "higher" and "lower" forms of pleasure found the former superior to the latter. His best-known example of this argument was that it was better to be "Socrates dissatisfied" than "a fool satisfied." This allowed Mill to resolve a challenge to Utilitarianism. Another argument of Mill's was that "The only proof... that an object is visible is that people actually see it... In like manner... the sole evidence... that anything is desirable is that people... desire it. If the end... the utilitarian doctrine proposes... were not, in theory and practice, acknowledged to be an end, nothing could ever convince any person... it was so." While some find this argument "notorious," it may have anticipated behavioral theory as a corollary to the concept that only observable actions, not internal states, can be described and measured. Mill equated people's desire for happiness with utilitarianism's aim of the overall good.

Mill maintained that, because people want to be happy individually, the Utilitarian goal of overall/general happiness is "a good to the aggregate of all persons." One critic (G. E. Moore, 1873-1958) criticized Mill's position as a "naïve and artless... use of the naturalistic fallacy." He found Mill's defense ambiguous in its basis: Moore claimed that "good" and "desirable" were not equal as Mill had argued. While Mill made the analogy between "visible" meaning "able to see" and "desirable" meaning "able to desire," Moore disagreed that these were the same. He made a distinction between what is and what should be, arguing that "desirable" did not mean what could be desired, but rather what "ought" or "deserves" to be desired. He also argued that "detestable," at the other extreme, did not mean what could be detested, but what "ought to be detested." However, Mill's argument was an alternative to Bentham's egalitarian ethic, which critics viewed as "swine morality" because he did not qualitatively discriminate between human and animal moral status and value.

Whereas Bentham's ethic was strictly consequential to the extent of considering morality only as instrumental instead of intrinsic, Mill departed from Bentham in this regard in viewing intrinsic factors as instrumental also, by emphasizing remorse, guilt, and other internal sanctions as effective for regulating human behavior. This emphasis was informed by Mill's view of human nature as social rather than only self-interested. In addition to people's caring about others, Mill found it caused people pain to harm others. Such pain generated negative self-perceptions, e.g., guilt. Furthermore, Mill found such internal sanctions just as important instrumentally as external punishments. In addition, Mill believed that the human conscience and sense of justice were natural psychological factors underlying human motivation. In *Utilitarianism*, Mill wrote that the natural human impulses for sympathy and self-defense were the sources of wanting to punish people who harm others, which desire contributes to the human sense of justice. While Mill found this sense a natural feeling, he also stated that justifying it by considering others' welfare in intelligent decision-making made it normatively appropriate.

Both Bentham and Mill applied utilitarian concepts for informing and reforming social and legal policy. When Mill upheld the value of freedom of speech and women's suffrage, he incorporated the utilitarian aim of promoting happiness as the foundation for their defense. While he agreed that people possess certain rights, he always returned to the point that social utility underlay such rights. If a supposed duty or right was found to cause harm, it was not a genuine one. Regarding women's suffrage, Mill argued that, in ideal marriages, equal partners with "cultivated faculties" influenced one another equally. He reasoned that, because women had the capacity for such cultivated faculties, denying their access to education, employment, voting, political office, and other opportunities was denying a significant means to happiness, hence the importance of raising women's social status. Moreover, he found men who denied women such opportunities had morally inferior motivations and pleasures. Bentham and Mill both criticized traditional social practices appealing to the natural order; they found appealing to utility instead correct.

Josiah Royce

Royce (1855-1916) was one of America's foremost champions of the metaphysical perspective of absolute idealism. Shared by Hegel and Bradley, this was the belief that a single inclusive consciousness united all parts of reality, even those we perceived as contradictory or unconnected. In addition to this school of thought, Royce contributed original ideas in the fields of ethics, logic, philosophy of religion, and philosophy of community. *The Religious Aspect of Philosophy* (1885), *The World and the Individual* (1899-1901), *The Philosophy of Loyalty* (1908), and *The Problem of Christianity* (1913) were included among his major publications. Royce and the famous philosopher and psychologist William James engaged in a long-term, amicable debate called "The Battle of the Absolute," profoundly affecting both men's thinking. In later writing, Royce discarded his earlier idealism's Absolute Mind in favor of a semiotically-based "absolute pragmatism," viewing reality as a universe of concepts, i.e., signs, existing within a process of interpretation by an endless community of minds—which community and minds themselves were also signs. This metaphysic is found in Royce's logic, ethics, philosophy of religion and philosophy of community.

Royce believed in an infinite being, which could be construed as Absolute Mind or as the infinite Community of Interpretation, and enabled understanding human life. He saw the infinite manifested in finite space, time, and individuals. This relationship of individuals to infinity, which Royce described in terms of loyalty, was his basis for ethics and religion. In *The Philosophy of Loyalty* he wrote of the rational relationship of human personal experience to "universal conscious experience." Royce analyzed the required conditions to make an individual's life meaningful, grounding his ethics in these. Moral conventions were insufficient for living with moral significance; individual will, expressed self-consciously through one's actions, which furthered realization of a life plan based on a goal chosen freely, was necessary. As the typical conflicts of individual impulses and wishes impeded a goal and attendant life plan, social experience provided these, mostly pre-formed by many people's contributions over time. A shared cause defined and focused individual will. Royce defined loyalty as morally relevant commitment to cause and community. Loyalties in turn explained moral life. Individual actions' community loyalty determined their moral value. Royce emphasized "loyalty to loyalty": individual loyalty must not undermine social/community loyalty.

Royce was among the first American philosophers to realize the significance of Nietzsche's moral philosophy in its challenge of approving autonomous individual wills' exercise to "socially idealized" powers. Ralph Waldo Emerson, William James, and poet Walt Whitman also championed this inspiring, "heroic" individualism; but Royce found it inadequate and ineffective in being so individual it lacked community loyalty. He found loyalty essentially social: Royce wrote (1913), "My life means nothing, either theoretically or practically, unless I am a member of a community." He believed the only way to be ethical individually was to choose and serve a cause, offering as examples the samurai to his master in feudal Japan and the knight to his lady in Medieval romances. Royce's logic identified community as preceding individual. He found social roles and causes defined by communities necessary to understanding concepts of personal identities and purposes. Community required not only groups of individuals, but also communication; cohesive will, thought, and sentiment; mutual history, or "community of memory"; and shared future expectations, or "community of hope," as bases for loyalty. Individuals retained their identities while also having a larger community life and guiding super-human personality or "Interpreting spirit."

Ayn Rand

Russian-American Rand (1905-1982), most famous for her novels *The Fountainhead* and *Atlas Shrugged,* developed a comprehensive philosophy of objectivism including an epistemological theory and a theory of art, expressed through essays and novels. She studied philosophy, including Plato, Aristotle, logic, Locke, the psychology of philosophy, Marx, Lenin, Hegel, Nietzsche, cinematography, and screenwriting. Her love of Victor Hugo's novels influenced the Romantic Realism of her own novels. At the beginning of her career, she authored short stories, stage plays, and screenplays. Her first novel, *We the Living* (1936), set in the post-revolutionary Soviet Union, was largely autobiographical. Before its publication, Rand received multiple publisher rejections for two years for its anti-Communist sentiments due to popular approval of the "Soviet experiment" among contemporary intellectuals. It subsequently sold over three million copies. Seeking a "kind of rest" from her work on *The Fountainhead* (1943), Rand wrote *Anthem* (1938), a dystopian novel. *The Fountainhead* was also rejected many times before publication due to its individualistic philosophy. Though its critical reviews were mostly negative, word of mouth made it a best-seller and Rand internationally famous. *Atlas Shrugged* (1958) cemented her renown, contributing to the official Objectivist movement including academic courses and journals.

Despite her pursuit of a strong interest in philosophy, Rand stated that her "life purpose" and great, first love was a kind of utopian social reform: "the creation of the kind of world... that represents human perfection." She insisted her interest in philosophy was "only" a means to this end. Regardless, following the publication of *Atlas Shrugged,* her crowning achievement in creating such an ideal world and her final fictional novel, Rand continued to write essays and give lectures in which she developed her ideas about rationality, ethical egoism, metaphysical realism, laissez-faire capitalism, individual rights, and art; and to apply her philosophical concepts to various social issues. Although Rand mostly rejected Libertarian politics, this movement has derived much inspiration from her moral defense of the minimal state which exists only to protect individual rights, and continues to do so. (A contemporary Libertarian philosopher, Robert Nozick, also championed the minimal state.) In spite of their non-academic popularity, Rand's works were only considered seriously by a few among professional philosophers.

Rand characterized ethics as a code of values for guiding the choices and actions that determined the purposes and courses of people's lives. She maintained that, before herself, no other philosopher had ever given a satisfactory code of ethics because none ever gave a scientific answer to the question of why people need such a code. Seeing value, or the classical Good, as what humans seek to obtain and retain, she found this presumed the idea of an "entity" that could accomplish a goal "in the face of an alternative," i.e., life or death. Values per se emerged from this conditional nature of life. She stated that, metaphysically, only life was an end in itself, "a value gained and kept by a constant process of action." What promoted life was good; what threatened it, evil. All real human values, e.g., ethics, philosophy, art, food, etc. were justified as necessary to survival. Thus Rand concluded that choosing to live equaled accepting one's life as one's "ethical purpose."

Rand rejected subjectivist philosophies, developing her own objectivist theory. She disagreed with intrinsicist approaches emphasizing inherent internal qualities. Rand greatly admired Aristotle, and agreed with his naturalist approach. Therefore she also disagreed as Aristotle did with Plato's ideas of forms that were independent of objects or beings. Her objectivism is compatible with Aristotle's empiricist view that all things can be explained through direct observation and evidence of natural phenomena. In contrast to Plato's concept of the Good as existing per se in the absolute, Rand agreed with Aristotle that the Good must always be instrumental, i.e., good *for* something. Rand's concept of morality's function both agreed and disagreed with Hobbes's idea: she agreed with Hobbes that morality was required for long-term survival, but she disagreed with his ideas that morality was basically social or needed a social contract. As beings whose survival depended on thinking and producing, humans would require morality even on a deserted island in Rand's view. Survival was not a moral obligation to Rand, but rather related to a hypothetical imperative, i.e., we must value morality as the means required to survive if we value our long-term survival, which we do if we choose to live.

Like Aristotle's ethics, Rand's ethics is teleological, i.e., related to life's ultimate purpose; and this-worldly, not otherworldly like Plato's. It is foundationalist, in contrast to David Hume and Adam Smith, who mistrusted foundationalist approaches for discrediting ordinary people's moral judgments in favor of theories created by intellectuals and preferred analysis and reform from within. Rand believed virtue was "not an end in itself" and "not its own reward." She believed a truly scientific code of ethics was based on concepts that reason is indispensable to human survival and our chief tool for surviving; that we choose to use reason, and therefore, that rationality is the chief moral virtue fundamental to all other virtues, including productivity. Many Objectivists credit Rand with solving the "is-ought" problem of moral philosophy by demonstrating the content of morality is determined by necessities for surviving long-term as a rational being; hence, anybody choosing to live ought to be moral. Rand described her meta-ethical belief that happiness is the psychological "result, reward and concomitant" of living morally, i.e., rationally as the only means for long-term survival, which was the ultimate goal. However, she also often wrote happiness was the ultimate goal in the same sense as Aristotle.

Consequential ethics

Virtue ethics philosopher Elizabeth Anscombe (1919-2001) coined the name "consequentialism" in her essay "Modern Moral Philosophy" (1958) as a derogatory term for the main error she perceived in some moral theories; however, the term then was adopted by proponents and opponents alike of this school of ethics. It is also called teleological ethics. Whereas deontology judges an action right or wrong by its character, not its outcome; and virtue ethics concentrates on the character of the actor, not the outcome or nature of the action; consequential ethics judges the morality of an action according to its outcome or consequence. This relates to "the end justifies the means." Consequential ethics theories must consider which consequences are good, who benefits from moral actions, and who judges consequences and how they judge them. Agent-neutral consequentialism disregards individual personal goals in evaluating actions to take. Agent-focused consequentialism considers individual, family, and friends' as well as general welfare. Types of consequentialism include Asceticism, Altruism, Egoism, Hedonism, Negative consequentialism, Rule consequentialism, and Utilitarianism. Epicureanism is a more moderate form of Hedonism; while seeking happiness, it defines happiness as tranquility rather than pleasure.

John Rawls

American liberal political philosopher Rawls (1921-2002) subscribed to the liberal tradition. In his theory of *justice as fairness*, he presented a vision of society composed of free citizens, all having equal fundamental rights and cooperating according to an economic system of egalitarianism. He described *political liberalism*, discussing how political power could legitimately be applied within a democracy and working to demonstrate that, regardless of the diverse worldviews enabled in free societies, they could still attain lasting unification. He further extended his theories to liberal foreign policy, aiming to envision an international system of tolerance and peace, in his writing about *the law of peoples*. Rawls was influenced by Norman Malcolm, a student of philosopher Wittgenstein, while studying at Princeton. Studying at Oxford, he worked with Isaiah Berlin, H. L. A. Hart, and Stuart Hampshire. He taught at Cornell, MIT, and for over 30 years at Harvard. In college he had considered priesthood, but fighting in World War II destroyed his Christian faith. His opposition to the war in Vietnam triggered his analysis of flaws in American politics. Some of his key works are *A Theory of Justice* (1971), *Political Liberalism* (1993), *The Law of Peoples* (1999), and *Justice as Fairness* (2001).

(1) Practically, political philosophy reveals grounds for a strongly divided society to reach agreement through reason. Rawls cites Hobbes' *Leviathan* as such an effort toward a solution for the problem of order in the English civil war, and the *Federalist Papers* (Hamilton, Madison, and Jay, 1787-1788) promoting the US Constitution's ratification. (2) Political philosophy helps people orient their social membership and political status within society, and understand their society's history and character from a broader viewpoint. (3) Political philosophy helps explore the boundaries of feasible political potential. It can describe political arrangements which real people will support and which can be implemented, and also imagine utopian social orders with ideal laws. (4) Political philosophy helps reconcile and "calm" people's "frustration and rage against our society and its history by showing us the way... its institutions... are rational, and developed over time... to... their present, rational form." By putting human foibles into a larger perspective, philosophy can demonstrate to people that life has improved in some ways. Rawls sought to contribute to reconciling democracy's long-term conflict of liberty vs. equality, and to delimiting civic and international tolerance.

To render all of one's beliefs—specific, general, and abstract—coherent and thereby justify them, Rawls cited reflective equilibrium as a criterion. In principle, any kind of belief could relate to conclusions regarding the arrangement of political institutions, e.g., epistemological beliefs about how we discover moral facts, or metaphysical beliefs about the personal identity or free will of people, etc. But in practice, Rawls maintained that moral and political theory that would be productive would be largely independent of epistemology or metaphysics in its development. Although traditional methodology assumed the priority of meta-ethical development, with moral and political theorizing as an outgrowth of meta-ethics, Rawls assigned the opposite sequence of priority, viewing meta-ethical progress as deriving from the progress previously attained in moral and political theory instead. Thus Rawls's theory of political liberalism subsequently gave rise to his meta-ethical theory of political constructivism regarding the validity and objectivity of political judgments.

Robert Nozick

American philosopher and Harvard professor Robert Nozick (1938-2002) was associated with the Libertarian and Analytic schools of political philosophy. He was also interested in ethics and epistemology, and wrote works on epistemology and decision theory. His best known book is *Anarchy, State, and Utopia* (1974), which won a National Book Award in the Philosophy and Religion category, and was a Libertarian response to the book of practical and utopian liberal political philosophy, *A Theory of Justice* by John Rawls. Some of his other works covering epistemology, metaphysics, axiology, and philosophy of science include *Philosophical Explanations* (1981), *The Examined Life* (1989), *The Nature of Rationality* (1993), *Socratic Puzzles* (1997), and *Invariances* (2001). His vast knowledge of mathematics, physics, economics, religion, psychology, and decision theory is evident from his writing. Nozick maintained that the chief criterion for evaluating state actions is respect for individual rights. Hence he found only a minimal state, limiting its activities to protecting life, liberty, property, and contract without using its power to make people moral, protect them from self-harm, or redistribute income, would be the only legitimate state.

Nozick based his particular form of Libertarianism upon a theory of natural rights, and on a related doctrine of acquired property rights. He found that ethics was composed of several layers. The first layer was an ethics of respect, formed of negative rights, i.e., things that a society should not require of its citizens. Nozick stated the only ethics that could be mandatory were the ethics of respect: "All that any society should (coercively) demand is adherence to the ethics of respect." In *Anarchy, State, and Utopia,* Nozick covered four chief topics: (1) the strength and nature of the moral rights underlying the book's primary normative structure; (2) the nature of and extent to which Nozick's defense of the minimal state succeeds against the individualist anarchist claim that "the state itself is intrinsically immoral"; (3) his defense and explication of his doctrine of justice in holdings by historical entitlement, and his related criticism of patterned and end-state distributive justice doctrines, particularly the difference principle espoused by John Rawls in *A Theory of Justice*; and (4) the argument that validating the minimal state is supported by utopian visions.

Nozick began *Anarchy, State, and Utopia* stating "individuals have rights, and there are things no person or group may do to them (without violating their rights)." Like John Locke and others, Nozick characterized such moral rights as state of nature rights: they are precursors and bases for evaluating and regulating individual, group, and legal and political institutional behavior. As Locke wrote that these rights are a law of nature or part of one, governing the state of nature before contracts and politics, Nozick also found them to precede social contracts. Such rights are not protected simply by social expedience: even socially optimal actions cannot be taken upon individuals by virtue of these rights, regardless how ideal the social goals of the actions. State of nature moral rights are negative in nature in that they proscribe doing certain things to individuals, instead of prescribing doing certain things for individuals. Not conferred by contracts, institutions, or for social goals, Nozick found these rights founded in exemplary moral facts of the natures of individuals as individuals. This individual rational dedication to moral purpose was, for Nozick, reason not to treat individuals as having to serve others' purposes.

Iain King

King, born 1971, is among the youngest persons ever knighted (2013) by the British Empire for work in Afghanistan, Kosovo, and Libya. A biography (Krznaric, 2012) states after graduating Oxford in 1993, he busked in Europe for a year "playing... guitar standing on his head." He was an early negotiator with Ireland's Sinn Féin following IRA cease-fire. He was UN peacekeeping administrator after Kosovo's 1998-1999 war, helped Kosovo adopt new currency, and was UN Head of Planning there in 2003. He co-authored a critically applauded book on Kosovo. He advised UN Secretary-General Kofi Annan regarding Africa. King was the civilian deployed to the most battle frontlines in Afghanistan, working with commanding officers and soldiers and surviving several Taliban attacks. During the Libyan civil war, he was deployed to Benghazi with 12 hours' notice, narrowly escaping death from a car bomb. He led the UK's conflict research program and democracy support agency, and managed the UN's Caribbean Disaster Relief Program. Despite work in 10 warzones, philosopher is King's main occupation. He taught philosophy at Cambridge and was associated with Blackburn's quasi-realism. His controversial ethics theory, influencing Buddhists, British Liberal Democrats, and public policy reform, is taught at some undergraduate colleges/universities.

King's philosophical writing and teaching are based on a combination of classical philosophy and insights drawn from his own experiences. He calls for a "revolution" in the field of ethics, analogous to the revolution in science brought by Sir Isaac Newton's laws of physics. He begins his discussion of reform in ethics by analyzing the utilitarian philosophy. He cites seven defects commonly identified in utilitarianism: (1) it can defeat itself; (2) it focuses on future events to the exclusion of significant history; (3) it accords power for making decisions to "questionable" agents; (4) it is unfair in discriminating among people; (5) it focuses on group concerns at the expense of individual needs; (6) it undermines telling the truth, being fair, and making promises; and (7) it does not provide any clear-cut rules. King bases these often-observed flaws on a fundamental premise that "the basic reason for following it is hollow." Further, King criticizes John Stuart Mill's proof of utilitarianism as not being logic. Following this criticism, King has attempted to reconstruct utilitarianism to eliminate these problems.

(1) Through evolution, King finds entrenched moral values have developed via environmental adaptation. He sees these as equally imperative as facts from evolution's necessity, impossible to discard. Common human instincts like abhorring murder amount to "shared moral law[s]." (2) Restructuring Pascal's Wager to eliminate religion, King proposes people should find value in life to make it meaningful. He finds accepting some obligations and having empathy with others necessary to seeking value, and using "proofs"—clear rationales/arguments, elucidated by multiple "thought-experiments"—to support these contentions. (3) King questions the qualities we should expect from our moral and decision-making system, concluding all systems must "provide a motive, be consistent [with themselves], and broadly consistent with our instincts." Only a virtue better matching these requirements than its opposite, equal virtue comprises the "essence of right and wrong." Obligation and empathy are the only qualities he finds meet these criteria, making them superior as bases for ethics to other evolved instincts. King calls obligation and ethics the "DNA of right and wrong." (4) Adapting John Rawls' principle into his own Help Principle (help somebody if it is worth more to them than you), King considers ethical rules people would use if self-interest were eliminated.

Feminist ethics

According to feminist philosopher Alison Jaggar ("Feminist Ethics", 1992), ethics from a uniquely female perspective endeavors to remedy five respects wherein traditional, male-oriented ethics devalues or disregards the feminine experience. (1) More interest in men's issues vs. less in those of women. (2) The trivialization of work in the home and caregiving for children, elders, and the ill primarily done by women. (3) The implication that women are somehow less profound and/or mature morally than men. (4) The underrating of culturally female characteristics such as life, the body, nature, imminence, emotion, sharing, connection, trust, interdependence, community, process, lack of hierarchy, peace, and joy; and the concomitant overrating of culturally male characteristics such as death, the intellect, culture, transcendence, asceticism, domination, wariness, independence, hierarchy, product, hierarchy, war, and will. (5) Traditional, male-oriented ethics demonstrates a bias of preferring masculine types of moral reasoning that place more emphasis on rights, rules, impartiality, and universality to the exclusion of less emphasis on feminine types of moral reasoning that place more emphasis on responsibilities, relationships, partiality, and specificity.

The primary purpose of feminist ethics is to establish a "gendered" ethics that removes, or at least mitigates, oppression of women especially and of any other social group. A diverse range of gender-focused approaches to ethics has been developed by feminists. These are all concerned with some of the manners in which traditional, male-oriented ethics has disregarded women. For example, some focus on caregiving and other behaviors and characteristics typically associated with women. Some focus more on the woman's status as what Simone de Beauvoir described as the second sex and its ideological, political, legal, and economic origins and outcomes. In the 18th and 19th centuries, John Stuart Mill, Mary Wollstonecraft (later Shelley), Catherine Beecher, Charlotte Perkins Gilman, Elizabeth Cady Stanton and others considered questions of "women's morality" including: whether physiology, psychology, cognition and affect were related to moral virtues as well as gender characteristics; whether "feminine" characteristics were biological/natural or socially conditioned; whether moral virtues differed along with gender traits between women and men; and whether people should operate based on an assumption of such a difference, or instead apply a "one-size-fits-all" morality to female and male human beings alike.

Continuing discussions of gender in ethics from 18th-century intellectuals like Mary Wollstonecraft, 19th-century thinkers viewed women as less intellectual but more moral than men, which some historians find ironic and John Stuart Mill found disturbing. As a utilitarian, Mill found it wrong for society to establish moral double standards for women and men. He believed society had systematically conditioned women to be morally superior: in *The Subjection of Women,* he wrote that women's self-denial was socially taught, not independently chosen. He found women were considered less strong and intelligent than men and hence were taught to defer to men, making their virtue not an autonomous choice but programmed by society. Mill insisted both sexes must comply equally with human standards of virtue to enable the most just and prosperous society. While first Wollstonecraft, then Mill, stressed egalitarian human virtue, diverse contemporaries of Mill's disagreed, believing virtue should be either "separate-but-equal" or separate-and-unequal, the latter finding female virtue inherently superior. But they disagreed about feminine traits like self-sacrificing, nurturing, empathy, kindness, and compassion, variously finding these real virtues all people should cultivate, positive psychological characteristics only women should cultivate, or negative psychological characteristics nobody should cultivate.

Rather than calling for a differentiation of ethics for women, Wollstonecraft characterized an egalitarian approach to human ethics as affirming women's equality with men. In *A Vindication of the Rights of Women*, she argued that women were not naturally morally "weak" as many of her contemporaries thought, but simply required the same rigorous education as men to develop their rationalism, which in turn would enable moral maturity. She attributed hypersensitivity, narcissism, over-emotionalism, and self-indulgence in women to being denied equal rational development. Wollstonecraft found reason, not feeling, as differentiating humans from other animals. She contended that parents in her day taught morals to boys but manners to girls. She found manners could be mastered automatically, whereas critical thinking was needed to master morals. She depicted society overall as impeding female moral growth by encouraging women to develop immaturity, vanity, cunning, and similar negative attributes. Moreover, Wollstonecraft found potential female virtues distorted into vices by society, e.g., positive gentleness into obsequiously submissive dependence. Though she described education as enabling women to provide men with more rational relationships, she also indicated women's need for economic independence from men to be "really virtuous and useful."

A 19th-century thinker, Catherine Beecher believed that "women's place was in the home"—not denying their rights as today's feminists might view it, but championing women's work as different but equally demanding as men's work: emphasizing the equal cognitive, occupational, and organizational skills required to manage a household as for managing a business, Beecher pioneered the "domestic science" discipline. Viewing women's establishment and maintenance of strong families supported by strong moral virtue as necessary to societal well-being, Beecher strove to teach society to accord women's work in the home the esteem it deserved. Also, from a religious perspective Beecher characterized women's roles as providing role models for developing Christ-like virtues in their family members, e.g., benevolence and self-denial. She saw women as positioned better than men by being in the home, insulated from the temptations of power, prestige, and wealth, for cultivating greater perfection and purity in themselves and hence in their families. Beecher believed that women's perfecting children and men morally would ultimately improve society.

Elizabeth Cady Stanton (1815-1902) noticed how female and male morality differed. Regarding the debate during her time whether these differences were biologically predetermined or socially conditioned, she was undecided. However, she felt men's morality had determined public behavior standards and also found it inferior. Unlike her approximate contemporary Catherine Beecher, who championed and elevated women's work in the home as a solution for social reform beginning from within the family, Stanton believed women and their superior morality should be moved from the home into public life, where their positive influence would be the solution to social reform. Both Beecher and Stanton were Christians and praised the benevolence and self-denial of women But Stanton emphasized women's self-development as well. She warned that, while charitable acts by women were laudable, they could also backfire by reinforcing women's secondary status. Stanton maintained that, rather than being entirely other-centered, women must also be self-centered at times to ensure self-care and obtain equal social, economic, and political powers and benefits as men enjoyed.

Poet and author Charlotte Perkins Gilman (1860-1935) was related to feminist ethicist Catherine Beecher and author Harriet Beecher Stowe (*Uncle Tom's* Cabin). Gilman wrote the famous, autobiographically-inspired short story, "The Yellow Wall-Paper" (1892) illustrating the effects of depression and ineffective/effective treatments. She founded the magazine *The Forerunner* (1909-1916) as a venue where she and others could write on social reform and women's issues. In addition to lecturing, Gilman wrote several non-fictional works furthering women's rights activism, including *Women and Economics* (1898), *The Home: Its Work and Influence* (1903), and *Does a Man Support His Wife?* (1915). Gilman depicted superior female morality in her fictional utopian novel *Herland* (1915), about an all-female society wherein private and public life differed dramatically from real society: with only women, things like individualism, competition, and domination did not exist. instead, cooperation produced higher morals as well as healthier psychological development. In this utopia, the highest human virtue incorporated both "feminine" and "masculine" virtues. In the real world, Gilman wrote in *Women and Economics* that economic inequality perpetuated male arrogance and female servility; women must be equal with men economically to develop self-respect, the human moral virtue perfectly combining humility and pride.

18th- and 19th-century feminist ethicists including Mary Wollstonecraft, John Stuart Mill, Catherine Beecher, Elizabeth Cady Stanton, and Charlotte Perkins Gilman contributed diverse approaches to ethics which defined a number of comparisons and contrasts between masculine and feminine perspectives. In the process, they initiated discussions of various underlying epistemologies and ontologies. These discussions provided challenges to the ontological assumption that the individual self is more fully developed when it is more separate from others. In addition, their conversations challenged the epistemological assumption that knowledge more accurately reflects reality when it is more rational, impartial, abstract, and universal. Both of these assumptions were common to traditional ethical approaches. In challenging these, the feminist ethicists of the 18th and 19th centuries proposed in their place the ontological assumption that the self is better developed and superior when it is more connected to others, rather than separate; and the epistemological assumption that knowledge more accurately reflects reality actually experienced by people when it is more emotional, partial, concrete, and specific. Therefore, 18th- and 19th-century feminist ethics eventually replaced the conceptual ideal of "autonomous man" with that of "communal woman."

In reworking ethical ontologies and epistemologies to reflect views of reality and knowledge from more feminine, less masculine perspectives, 18th- and 19th-century feminist ethicists eventually came to view the ideal of the "communal woman" in lieu of the "autonomous man." As 20th-century feminist ethicists built upon these foundations established by their predecessors, they developed diverse feminist approaches to ethics focused on care. Specifically feminist care-focused approaches to ethics differ from care-focused approaches to ethics that are not explicitly feminist in that non-feminist care-focused approaches view ethics from the orienting perspective of care, but are not concerned with gender issues, whereas the feminist approaches are significantly sensitive to gender issues. In contrast to other care-focused ethicists, feminist care-focused ethicists typically observe and call attention to ways in which patriarchal societies tend to relegate females to subordinate status, and often fail to accord feminine ways of thinking, loving, working, and writing the equal esteem that they are due.

Carol Gilligan, Nel Noddings, and other feminist care ethicists find that, to the extent that traditional moral principles, theories, policies, and practices omit, disregard, demean, or minimize cultural virtues and values viewed as typically feminine, they are deficient to the same extent. Sigmund Freud viewed moral development according to his theory of psychosexual development. Freud theorized that innate fear of castration by their fathers forced boys to sever their early-childhood attachment to their mothers. However, absent this exclusively male threat of castration anxiety, he believed girls continued to be attached to their mothers. Therefore, Freud believed females developed a sense of autonomous moral agency much more slowly. This sense of moral autonomy equated to recognizing one's personal responsibility for the consequences of one's actions relative to society's rules and laws, i.e., either obey its rules or be subject to its punishments. To Freud, this meant that females ultimately did not grow to respect societal laws as strongly as males; hence he found females morally "inferior" to males. Gilligan criticized Freud and many other traditional intellectuals for this view. She found feminine morality different from masculine morality, not inferior to it.

As a corollary to his highly influential theory of cognitive development, Jean Piaget proposed a theory of moral development. He theorized younger children reasoned in terms of heteronomous morality, i.e., judging behaviors by their consequences, not their intentions, and viewing rules as immutable; and older children in terms of autonomous morality, i.e., considering intentions as well as consequences, and viewing rules as conventions that could be changed circumstantially. Piaget described preadolescent/early adolescent morality as that of cooperation and reciprocity among people; and also identifying some actions as wrong irrespective of outcome. He described middle/later adolescent morality as "ideal reciprocity," i.e., considering others' perspectives to inform decision-making, or the Golden Rule. Lawrence Kohlberg developed a Piaget-based theory of moral development, as influential among morality theories as Piaget's cognitive-developmental theory was among cognitive theories. Kohlberg's three levels incorporate six stages: the Pre-Conventional level includes Stage 1, Punishment and Obedience Orientation; and Stage 2, Instrumental Purpose/Relativist Orientation. The Conventional level includes Stage 3, Morality of Interpersonal Cooperation ("Good Boy-Nice Girl"); and Stage 4, Social-Order-Maintaining Orientation ("Law and Order"). The Post-Conventional level includes Stage 5, Social-Contract/Legalistic Orientation; and Stage 6, Universal Ethical Principle Orientation.

Gilligan acknowledged the widespread acceptance of Kohlberg's theory, but did not feel this necessarily indicated its veracity. She questioned whether Kohlberg's moral developmental stages were as unvarying as he proposed (and as Piaget before him proposed his cognitive developmental stages were), as universal, and necessarily existed in the same hierarchical order. A major problem Gilligan identified with Kohlberg's theory was that, in experiments/surveys, women seldom surpassed his third stage while men typically reached his fourth or fifth stage. She proposed rather than lesser female moral development, this indicated inherent gender bias in his methodology. As males, subscribing to male-oriented traditional ethics, Gilligan said Kohlberg and his researchers spoke the language of justice, emphasizing rules and rights. From studying women's reflections on abortion-related decisions, Gilligan concluded women spoke a language of care, emphasizing responsibilities and relationships instead. In *A Different Voice* (1982), Gilligan pointed out that women's different moral language would inaccurately place them lower on Kohlberg's male-oriented scale of moral development.

In his theory of moral development, Kohlberg proposed three general levels of moral reasoning: Pre-Conventional, Conventional, and Post-Conventional. These closely mirrored Piaget's levels of cognitive development: young children were Pre-Operational, not yet able to perform mental operations; middle children were Concrete Operational, able to perform mental operations but only concerning concrete objects and events; and pre-adolescents, adolescents and adults were Formal Operational, able to perform abstract mental operations about purely abstract concepts and hypothetical situations without the aid of concrete referents. Kohlberg's Pre-Conventional level included the obedience/punishment and instrumental relations typical of young children's intuitive thinking that Piaget described. His Conventional level included the cooperative and legalistic morality typical of Piaget's Concrete Operations. Kohlberg's Post-Conventional level attained the universal ethical principles enabled by Piaget's abstract thought. Whereas Kohlberg's levels view morality relative to rules/laws, Gilligan's moral levels represent relational ethics. Her first level reflects self-interest, her second level other-interest, and her third combines both into a relational unit. The interdependence of Gilligan's third level constitutes fully feminist thinking.

Some critics maintain that, despite care being a true moral virtue, justice is a more essential one. Their common argument is that more universal moral principles like helping the needy

- 35 -

Copyright © Mometrix Media. You have been licensed one copy of this document for personal use only. Any other reproduction or redistribution is strictly prohibited. All rights reserved.

are more reliable and superior for guiding action than transitory emotions of caring for particular individuals. This accompanies a belief that impartiality should resolve conflicts between care and justice; e.g., essential needs and rights are equal for all children without considering one's own children above others. Another criticism is that Kohlberg's theory describes men's moral development and Gilligan's describes women's, hence neither describes overall human moral development. Gilligan has responded to this by studying male moral experiences, exploring how American society encourages male competition for public success—stifling males' moral sensitivity and nurturing potential. She points out that, even though women today are almost as fluent in the masculine justice-oriented moral language as in their feminine care-oriented moral language, males today still have great difficulty expressing moral considerations in anything other than masculine terms. Gilligan illustrates in these studies the significance for informing moral decisions of feminist Level Three thought incorporating self-care and other-care into relational morality.

While Gilligan's "Different Voice" ethics is that of care instead of justice, some criticize that traditional (i.e., male-dominated) ethics contains equal benevolence, which they equate with Gilligan's care, as justice. Their examples include not harming others, maximizing the collective good, and not limiting individual liberties as emerging from benevolence, while legal equality and equal personal respect emerge from justice. However, a flaw in their criticism may be equating Gilligan's definition of care with the traditional notion of benevolence. Philosopher Lawrence A. Blum makes this distinction. As an example, he distinguishes the general principle of benevolence, the source of the specific principle to protect one's children from harm, from the actual quality of caring: although most parents believe in protecting their children from harm, Blum finds only parents aware of and sensitive to their children's unique needs and interests—i.e., caring parents—are able to know how and when to do so.

Some critics of Carol Gilligan's feminist ethics of care argue that it is no different from the concept of benevolence found in traditional ethics. However, philosopher Lawrence A. Blum (*Friendship, Altruism, and Morality,* 1980) makes the distinction between traditional benevolence as guiding moral action, using the example of parents' believing the general principle of protecting their children from harm, and Gilligan's care as informing parents' ability to implement that principle through their specific knowledge of what their own children need and want. Many traditional philosophers agree with Blum that caring parents tend to behave benevolently more than uncaring ones, but they disagree that only caring parents are capable of benevolent action. They believe a formal sense of duty is enough to cause moral behavior, with or without caring. However, Blum and others developing various care ethics find the sense of duty (e.g., to obey our society's laws) is not sufficient alone for acting morally. They believe parents and others must additionally have appropriate feelings of care to take fully moral actions.

Among feminist criticisms of Gilligan's feminist care ethic, those with particular impact state that, even though women have demonstrated better caring than men, it can constitute poor epistemological, ethical, and political judgment to associate the value of care explicitly with women. Some critics warn that connecting care and women carries the danger of encouraging the belief that women are "in charge of" caring; and/or the idea that, as superior carers, women must care at their own expense. For example, Sandra Lee Bartky (*Femininity and Domination,* 1990) contends that women have been disempowered by experiences of tending to men's injuries and massaging male egos. She describes the "emotional work" that women in service professions practice as responsible for women's disconnection from their own emotional moorings. An example is employers' requiring women to present positive faces regardless of whether clients/patients/customers are hostile, abusive, or rude: continuing inauthentic "nice" behavior undermines the ability to distinguish whether such behavior is real or faked.

Many women have affirmed meaningfulness in their roles of caring for children, husbands, and others, including when challenging. While some women feel emotionally drained by personal/professional emotional work, others find it energizing. The latter women experience increasing self-images as the "glue" for everybody in their lives, in proportion to their increasing care for others. While feminist ethicist Sandra Lee Bartky, who criticizes Carol Gilligan's feminist care ethics as inherently dangerous to women, acknowledges some women feel empowered by caring, she points out these feelings are subjective and not equal to objective power in reality. As one example, many women worry much more about men's feelings than men do about women's feelings. Whereas these women strive to please men and feel upset if they fail, in many cases the men are oblivious to the emotional impacts of what they say and do on the women. Bartky therefore finds care of men by women can constitute a "collective genuflection by women to men, an affirmation of male importance that is unreciprocated" (*Femininity and Domination*, 1990).

Sandra Lee Bartky (*Femininity and Domination*, 1990) takes issue with Carol Gilligan's proposed ethics of female care in contrast to traditional male-oriented ethics of justice. In addition to the potential of women's care of men for disempowering women, for causing women to disconnect from their own emotions, and for promoting care that is not reciprocal, Bartky also warns women can care for men at the expense of their own moral integrity. She illustrates using the example of Fritz Stangl, the Kommandant of the Nazi extermination camp Treblinka during World War II, and his wife Teresa. Teresa Stangl knew her husband ordered the murders of thousands of Jewish people among millions killed, yet she loved him and fulfilled her wifely duties by caring for his needs. Bartky contends Teresa Stangl's care of her husband constituted complicity with his evil deeds. She writes a woman cannot expect to preserve her own goodness unaffected while silent about her knowledge her husband's evildoing. Thus Bartky warns women that, before fully embracing any care ethics, they must consider the "pitfalls and temptations of caregiving itself."

Like Sandra Lee Bartky (*Femininity and Domination*, 1990), Sheila Mullet ("Only Connect: The Place of Self-Knowledge in Ethics," 1987) sees inherent dangers for women in embracing Carol Gilligan's ethics of care. Mullet makes a distinction between "undistorted caring" vs. "distorted caring." In other words, if a woman is economically, socially, or psychologically forced to care for somebody, she is not able to provide true care. For example, if women are dominated by and subordinate to men, authentic caring of men by women is impossible. Mullet defines care that is appropriate is performed well and reflectively. She finds that both women and men will be morally deprived when women provide more caregiving than their fair share. While caring too much poses the danger of servility, caring too little poses the threat of becoming overly selfish, which "freezes" the heart. When women and men are not equal, women's care of men is accompanied by fear that men will not feel any need to reciprocate and will take advantage of women's caring. However, if women and men are truly equal, women can care for men without these fears.

In response to Lawrence Kohlberg's theory of moral development, which seemed to produce gender-biased results when examining levels of morality in women vs. men, Carol

Gilligan studied women's moral decisions and concluded that, while traditional ethics reflect a male justice orientation, female ethics reflect a care orientation instead. Other feminist ethicists like Sandra Lee Bartky and Sheila Mullet then found cause for concern that, instead of validating the "Different Voice" of women that Gilligan identified, the ethics of care could backfire by reinforcing gender inequality in a number of different ways, including lack of reciprocity, mandating and/or untenably intensifying women's already caring roles, female complicity in male immoral actions via women's care of men, etc. However, philosophy scholars find that, without discrediting the attention Bartky's and Mullet's warnings deserve, Gilligan's work, as well as the feminist care ethic in general, still hold merit. Rather than being grounds to reject the care ethic, the arguments about it are grounds for developing a stronger feminist care ethic including both women and men. Gilligan's additional research with men has made inroads in this respect and can be continued.

Consistently with Carol Gilligan's emphasis on relationships rather than rights as the center of feminist ethics, Noddings responded to the need to enhance feminist care ethics by developing a code of ethics championing values and virtues that tradition has associated with females. The relationships she characterizes ethics as concerning are those between the "one-caring" and the one "cared-for." Noddings particularizes the subject of care, finding true value and virtue in caring for the specific individuals in one's life rather than in abstractly declaring universal love from afar for humanity in general. She also finds specific care for real individuals more relevant than impersonal donations to help disaster or war victims. Noddings asserts that caring and wanting to help others come naturally to us as children. When, as busy adults, we find our commitments interfere with such natural caring, she describes deliberate, ethical caring as compensating. However, she finds ethical caring, though valuable, less fundamental than natural caring: the latter enables and is prerequisite to the former.

In *Caring: A Feminine Approach to Ethics and Moral Education* (1984), Noddings maintains men have the ability and duty to care, yet uses women as caregiver examples most frequently. Some critics object that Noddings upholds care by women such that it endangers women's own integrity, identity, and survival. However, Noddings replies this is a misinterpretation. She believes self-care first is important for women—even though some find she regards this as necessary primarily to enable caring for others. Noddings places especial significance on maintaining relationships. She finds it concerning for people to sever relationships, especially close ones, without making every effort to preserve them, seeing the potential to be "ethically diminished" by such actions. Applying her care ethics principles to public policy in *Starting at Home: Caring and Social Policy* (2002), Noddings answers critics who find feminist care ethics limited to domesticity. She maintains that moral lessons learned privately are foundations for a sense of wider social justice. She believes we should start at home, the source of care, to develop social policies for addressing education, mental illness, homelessness, and other issues most effectively.

Nel Noddings has applied feminist care ethics to public policy, saying that effective social reform begins in the home as the origin of caring. Fiona Robinson has extended this concept further by stating that policymakers can only achieve progress with social problems like poverty through a lens of critical feminist care ethics. To support this point, Robinson observes in *Globalizing Care: Ethics, Feminist Theory, and International Relations* (1999) that traditional ethicists have long sought to induce countries to eliminate the world's enormous income disparities using moral philosophies based on justice, duty, and rights—

unsuccessfully. She attributes this failure to the general, abstract nature of traditional ethics, which she finds mismatched with the specific nature of poverty and similar social problems. Robinson maintains that action to alleviate suffering cannot be motivated by such abstract approaches; instead, ethics must make affluent people conscious of poverty as part of their daily lives, enabling them to comprehend the relationship of their affluence with others' poverty. Robinson notes occasional charitable donations do less to relieve suffering than make the affluent feel good about themselves; she finds that sacrificing some advantages to influence social, political, and economic change would be more effective.

Three feminist ethicists sharing several common views with Gilligan and Noddings are Sara Ruddick, Virginia Held, and Eva Feder Kittay. One uniting factor is their belief that human relationships are not formed between equals in terms of their respective power and knowledge, but between interdependent and unequal individuals. For example, parent-child relationships involve different levels of power and knowledge. Even relationships between people the same age, e.g., teenagers, demonstrate power differentials, as when a well-adjusted, self-confident teen offers comfort, sympathy and advice to a friend who is distraught or depressed. Personal relationships involve variable levels of personal empowerment who try together to resolve issues concerning both—unlike interactions between businesspeople negotiating contracts. Ruddick, Held, and Kittay hence are of the opinion that the everyday experiences of most people—e.g., mothering and parenting practices, which represent moral dynamics best, should serve as models for establishing ethical systems rather than contractual and business concepts, images, and metaphors.

Feminist ethicists who take status-oriented approaches are first concerned with domination and subordination, i.e., issues of power, prior to considering care vs. justice, good vs. evil, and maternal vs. paternal thought. Both groups are equally feminist; however, their emphases lie in different areas. Systematic male subordination of females is addressed in various manners by status-oriented feminist ethicists. These diverse explanations and solutions for the second-sex status of women include liberal feminism, radical, Marxist/socialist, multicultural and global, ecological, existentialist, psychoanalytic, postmodern, and third-wave feminism. One common theme that runs through all of these feminist moral philosophies is the idea that, in order to establish true gender equality, all practices, institutions, structures, and systems that produce or perpetuate pervasive power disparities between the sexes must first be destroyed. Some scholars therefore opine that, contrary to Virginia Held and other care-based feminist ethicists, the status-oriented feminist ethicists view justice as taking precedence over care.

Mary Wollstonecraft's *Vindication of the Rights of Women,* "The Subjection of Women" by John Stuart Mill, and the 19th-century women's suffrage movement are historically the foundations of liberal feminist ethics. Today, the National Organization of Women (NOW) is one of the organizations most associated with liberal feminism. According to liberal feminists, governmental laws and established social norms impeding women's public success are the main reasons why women are subordinate to men. Liberal feminists maintain women cannot fulfill their potential in government, medicine, academics, business, etc. unless they have all of the same opportunities that men have. Proponents advise many people they are mistaken to presume the issues concerning liberal feminism have been addressed: NOW's 1967 Bill of Women's Rights is still not completely implemented, the Equal Rights Amendment has never been passed, American women's reproductive rights are still threatened, women earn less than men on average, and female Fortune 500 CEOs and female US Senators are minorities. Dependency/caregiving work, primarily done by women, receives among the lowest pay and status. These issues document the liberal feminist view that their continuing work remains substantial.

Radical feminists find liberal feminism misdirected in emphasizing equal pay for equal/comparable work, maternity leave, and similar affirmative actions. They believe only women's complete control of their sexual appetites and reproductive powers will change their second-sex status. Historically, radical feminists espoused libertarian approaches to sexuality and reproduction, encouraging ethically controversial sexual experimentation, childbirth surrogacy, and androgyny as antidotes to women's social inequality. These views evolved in time to be replaced by cultural feminism, which discarded libertarian attitudes but found heterosexuality an institution intended to objectify and control female sexuality for male gratification. Technologies enabling artificial reproduction were viewed by cultural feminists as ultimately making women sex objects through depriving them of their reproductive power. Cultural feminism rejected the former libertarian ideal of androgyny as attempting to be like males, finding feminine traits superior. Though its libertarian and cultural polar extremes are problematic, radical feminism overall has contributed valuable ethical thought.

While lesbian ethics has enriched feminist ethics, a primary source of controversy is its development in the service of only lesbian women or mainly women-centered women. Sarah Lucia Hoagland (*Lesbian Ethics,* 1989) characterizes lesbian ethics as not considering whether an individual/action is good, but rather whether it furthers one's liberation, freedom, and self-creation. Marilyn Frye ("A Response to Lesbian Ethics: Why Ethics?", 1999) adds that traditional ethics stresses not only being good oneself, but also making others good. This attitude that one is right and thus knows what is right for others is found quintessentially male by these feminist philosophers. They counter lesbian ethics seeks good only for oneself, not imposing it on others. Its emphasis on choice extends to making a chosen action/object good via free choice. Critics' primary problem with lesbian ethics is morally justifying actions via freely choosing them. Hoagland responds that society's extensive restrictions of lesbian choices warrant their emphasizing choice. She finds that, in choosing for themselves, lesbians mutually choose for each other in interactive moral agency. This oppression-resistant "lesbian context" provides personal meaning, i.e., moral value. Hence lesbian ethics concerns human development that avoids being dominated or dominating others.

Marxist/Socialist feminism primarily opposes liberal feminism, finding it impossible or highly difficult for women and other oppressed groups to succeed in social class systems. They believe replacing capitalist economic systems with socialist ones paying both sexes equally for equal work is the only way to eliminate female subordination. They find economic equality of the genders a prerequisite to their equal power. Departing from traditional Marxist beliefs that lower female social status is determined only by whether they are part of the workforce or not, contemporary Marxist/Socialist feminists have integrated into their theory and practice many concepts from radical feminism, and instead attribute gender inequality to multiple causes. For example, Juliet Mitchell (*Women's Estate,* 1971) identifies four socioeconomic factors that excessively affect women's status: sexuality, reproduction, the socialization of children, and women's role in production. Mitchell finds women's roles relative to all these must change to enable gender equality. In *Psychoanalysis and Feminism* (1974), Mitchell additionally cites psychic transformation as a requisite: exterior changes must be accompanied by women's conviction of their own worth.

While multicultural feminists generally agree with most views expressed by other feminist ethics regarding women's social status, they criticize and contribute to these schools of thought by calling attention to the concept that systems and structures related to race and class as well as gender are ultimately inextricable, which they find other approaches to feminist ethics have not considered adequately. Rather than attending exclusively to the oppression of females as women, or employees, or members of a disadvantaged racial/ethnic group, multicultural feminists say feminist ethicists should realize women's social status is determined by all their characteristics, e.g., race, income, sexuality, age, etc. They maintain although sexism, racism, classism, ageism, etc. can be separated in theory, they cannot be separated in reality. As bell hooks (real name Gloria Jean Watkins) writes, "interlocking systems of oppression" make many women victims of "multiple jeopardy" (*Yearning: Race, Gender, and Cultural Politics,* 1990), e.g., a Hispanic, undocumented, female, low-paid domestic for a highly-paid, white, female attorney. Such multiple sources of oppression can undermine self-image and identity, causing psychological and spiritual as well as material damages.

Global and postcolonial feminists give mainly laudatory responses to multicultural feminism. However, they still find this school of thought relatively incomplete in addressing the oppression of women by focusing overly on their own countries' gender politics. For example, mainly Northern Hemisphere, First-World nations like America overlook the social status and problems of women in mainly Southern Hemisphere, Third-World countries. Global feminists point out disparities, such as American feminists' efforts to promote laws against workplace sexual harassment while women in other countries suffer genital mutilation and being stoned to death for adultery. American feminists protest some pharmacists' conscientious objections against abortion impeding some women's obtaining emergency contraception while many more women in other countries die from mismanaged/unmanaged pregnancy, childbirth, and abortion, lacking access to family planning services. Moreover, postcolonial feminists point out not only material and economic disparities between First-World and Third-World women, but also the profit and privilege of First-World women at the expense of Third-World Women, paid slave wages to manufacture goods First-World women buy; or providing them low-paid services as nannies, servants, or homecare aides as exports to First-World nations.

While supporting global and postcolonial feminists regarding the diverse needs of women, ecofeminists emphasize human responsibilities to animals they find other feminist ethics have overlooked. For example, some ecofeminists have used Carol Gilligan's feminist ethics of care as the foundation for developing animal ethics. As noted by Peter Singer (*Animal Liberation,* 1974) and Tom Regan (*The Case for Animal Rights,* 1983), just as feminist ethics developed emphasizing care, relationships and responsibilities in reaction to traditional ethics emphasizing justice, rules, and rights, feminist animal care theory also developed in reaction to animal ethics based on rights and utilitarianism. As feminists found male-oriented ethics inadequate to explain women's needs, ecofeminists found human-oriented animal rights ethics inadequate to explain animals' needs. As critics find rationalistic ethics unsuitable to feminine morality by ignoring care and relationship in favor of justice and rights, critics of rights-based animal defense ethics find these explicitly repress/deny emotions in moral decisions regarding animals. Donovan and Adams (*Feminist Care Tradition in Animal Ethics,* 2007) observe that, because lack of emotion regarding animal suffering perpetuates animal abuse, care should apply to ethical animal treatment. Josephine Donovan finds feminist relational/care ethics should inform animal ethics.

Ecofeminists attribute the injustices, great socioeconomic disparities, and lack of care that are evident globally today to the human race's unconscious, indifferent, or even contemptuous treatment of our own environment. By consuming finite energy resources as if they were in infinite supply, polluting the air and water with toxic wastes, slaughtering animals as sources of meat that we eat in excess of what we need and to the detriment of our own health, stockpiling weapons of mass destruction, etc., we demonstrate a human belief in dominating nature. Ecofeminists (cf. Ynestra King, "Healing the Wounds: Feminism, Ecology, and Nature/Culture Dualism." 1995) find our belief that our efforts to control nature for our own benefit are a human right for shaping the world to make it better for our own lives are actually delusional: they are backfiring, as our destruction of the world's flora and fauna will ultimately doom us as well.

As Simone de Beauvoir wrote in her landmark work *The Second Sex* (1949), men designated man as Self and woman as Other. With Other being a threat to Self, women are then seen as threats to men. Thus men subordinate women to preserve male freedom and to make women believe that they do not deserve to be treated any better. Therefore, women need to acknowledge themselves as autonomous beings with the freedom of agency to decide their own fates in order to become real Selves in their own right. Existentialist feminist ethicists, instead of focusing on the physical and material outcomes of women's second-sex status, concentrate on the psychological outcomes for women of this status. Just as existentialist philosophy in general advocates defining one's existence independently of the terms of contexts which are deemed irrelevant, existentialist feminists maintain that women should also decide their own courses in life independently of male-dictated contexts, rather than defining themselves in terms of men or according to men's terms.

Both existentialist and psychoanalytic feminists look into women's psyches to explain women's status. With women predominantly raising children, girls and boys are socialized differently. Associating feminine cultural values with mothers and sisters, boys differentiate by separating from these, while girls retain connection to and emulation of mothers. Because patriarchal systems influence human values, children associate "feminine" values like care and kindness with nature, and "masculine" values like justice and conscientiousness with culture. Freudian psychosexual concepts reinforce viewing women as less valuable than men. Some psychoanalytic feminists attribute these erroneous views to our society's dependence on women for caregiving and men for world-building. They say if men spent as much time fathering as women do mothering, and women worked publicly as much as men, children would stop associating home with women and work with men, and see parents as valuing home and work equally. Other psychoanalytic feminists, however, think changing female status requires rejecting the necessity of resolving the Oedipus complex to emerge from the state of nature, relegating women to periphery and subordination. They say that, if women embrace mother-child symbiotic unity instead of men's "Symbolic Order," and celebrate their femaleness and live on their own terms, then patriarchy will disintegrate.

Postmodern and third-wave feminists reject any one explanation of women's oppression. As unique individuals, women cannot be labeled as a group or entity in their view. They associate any such insistence on only one absolute truth or reality with male thinking and patriarchal systems. Postmodern and third-wave feminists find that women must share their individual differences with one another. This will support their resistance against rigid, patriarchal, eternal "truth." In the view of postmodern and third-wave feminist ethics,

- 42 -

Copyright © Mometrix Media. You have been licensed one copy of this document for personal use only. Any other reproduction or redistribution is strictly prohibited. All rights reserved.

women need not follow a predetermined script, whether imposed by others or by themselves; rather, they must embrace their inherent contradictions and conflicts to become themselves. Feminist ethics, rather than dictating any unitary normative standards, provide women with many ways of understanding how their moral decisions are influenced by gender, race, class, age, etc. While non-feminist criticisms find them "female-based," traditional ethics that have assumed their own universality are actually male-based. Feminist ethics not only compensate for this imbalance, but moreover stimulate rethinking ethics to eliminate dominating, subordinating patterns demoralizing everybody. Scholars expect 21st-century globalization will challenge feminist ethics to further advances.

Ethical Analysis of Issues and Practical Applications

Morality

Morality can be defined descriptively or normatively. Descriptively, it can mean a set of codes for conduct that a given society has established, that a religion or other institution or group has established, or that an individual person has adopted for his or her own behavior. A conduct code found most important by any group or individual can define morality. Normatively, it can mean a code of behavior that all reasoning people would endorse under certain circumstances. When philosophers construct ethical theories, the meaning of the term "morality" makes a critical contribution, though this frequently goes unstated. One fundamental ethical question is whether a universal human morality exists or whether morality is relative to different groups of people. Logically, defining morality as a specific, real code of conduct that exists, established by a certain society or societies, negates the concept of a universal morality applicable to all people. Such a specific definition is a descriptive one, as employed by anthropologists in studying certain societies for characterizing their moralities. Some evolutionary and comparative psychologists identify morality or its close approximation among non-human animals.

Normative (rather than descriptive) meanings of morality are commonly assumed to describe a code of conduct applicable to everybody able to comprehend it. Normatively, morality is assumed to be accepted by all rational people under given, plausible conditions. It is also regarded as something never to be violated for non-moral reasons: normatively, nobody should ever fail to do what morality requires or do what it prohibits. Various types of moral theories exist according to what they represent as the circumstances wherein every rational individual would embrace a given code of conduct as a moral code, and to which characteristics they identify as being central features of rational individuals. These variations determine related variations in moral theories concerning to which individuals and their behaviors moral judgments apply. Some theories find morality applicable only to rational humans with traits like vulnerability and fallibility, which make embracing morality rational. Other moral theories apply morality to all rational beings with or without human traits—for example, including God.

A central feature of the descriptive meaning of morality not found in the normative meaning of morality is that descriptively, morality signifies codes of conduct that an existing individual, group, or society has established and endorses. Therefore, any other individual and anybody who is not a member of that group or society is not subject to that morality and need not behave accordingly. However, if a person accepts a normative definition of a given moral theory, i.e., its definitions of which beings are rational and under which conditions all such rational beings would identify a code of conduct as a moral code, that person is then committed to viewing certain behaviors as immoral. This could include behaviors in which the person might be tempted to engage. Since making such a commitment is a part of accepting a normative definition of morality, it follows that there are major disagreements among philosophers regarding which normative definition should be accepted.

An ambiguity in the meaning of morality is that, in its original descriptive definition, morality as a code of conduct must have been issued by a society and accepted by that society's members as a behavioral guide; but in its normative definition, morality is universal, and may not necessarily be issued by any society, group, or individual. One thing that both the descriptive and normative definitions of morality share in common is the concept that morality's behavioral guidance includes the principle of averting and eschewing harm to others. For thinkers who believe a universal code of behavioral norms exists, not every society includes a code of conduct having characteristics that meet the definition of a morality—in either the normative or descriptive meaning. These people would also agree that even societies having such codes that do meet these definitions often or always have "defective" moralities, i.e., not all rational individuals would support them completely. Natural law theorists, e.g., secular like Hobbes or theological like Aquinas, find all rational people know generally what morality allows and disallows—the former via natural reason, the latter via divinely endowed knowledge.

Morality, etiquette, and law

When morality is considered in a descriptive sense, it sometimes includes etiquette, though applying to relatively less serious behavioral norms. For example, in *Leviathan*, Thomas Hobbes' discussion of manners describes the most common traditional view of the types of behavioral norms included in a fundamental conception of morality: "By manners I mean not... decency of behavior, as how one man should salute another, or... wash his mouth or pick his teeth before company, and such other points of small morals, but those qualities of mankind that concern their living together in peace and unity." Distinctions between moral and legal systems include that laws are written, explicit rules with penalties for infractions, accompanied by officials designated to interpret and enforce these laws and apply the penalties specified. Commonalities include that morality and law frequently govern the same behaviors, moral principles are often used for evaluating laws, and changes in laws are frequently supported by moral criticism. Some authors (cf. Dworkin) also insist that morality must be employed in interpreting laws.

Morality and religion

One primary difference religions have from moral systems is that religions justify and/or explain the behaviors they prescribe and proscribe through stories they contain about past events, typically including deities and/or other supernatural entities. Some religions dictate codes of conduct that are not distinguished from moral codes. Moral and religious conduct codes frequently overlap substantially. However, some religions also can differ from moral systems, both by prescribing and/or proscribing more behaviors and by allowing other behaviors than moral systems. In some cases, morality is viewed as a religion's established code of conduct; even when it is not, many times morality is viewed as needing to be explained and justified by religion. While morality serves to guide people's behavior, religions always encompass more than behavioral guidelines. Similarly to the way laws can be criticized for moral reasons, some religious precepts and practices, for example discrimination based on gender, sexual orientation, or race, are criticized on the grounds of morality.

Carol Gilligan and Lawrence Kohlberg's theories of moral development

While Gilligan's theory originally deemed Kohlberg's theory based on a male morality consisting of a justice ethic of rules and rights, and countered this by proposing a female morality consisting of a care ethic of relationships and responsibilities, the two came to collaborate on the original just community project featuring democratic educational interventions, setting the standard for all ensuing such projects, each bringing their own perspectives on moral development. As Donald R. C. Reed (*Following Kohlberg: Liberalism and the Practice of Democratic Community,* 1998) observed, within four years after Gilligan published *In a Different Voice* (1982) outlining her feminist care ethics, "Kohlberg and Gilligan both revised their accounts of moral development so... they converged far more than... commonly recognized." Thus they not only contributed different perspectives to the just community project, they also influenced one another's views on moral development. Reed found the accords Kohlberg and Gilligan reached, and the insights gained through the just community efforts, could inform extending relationship ethics principles to deliberative democracy, wherein true deliberation and consensus go beyond voting and majority rule in democratic lawmaking decisions.

As a developmental psychologist, Kohlberg formulated a Piagetian theory of moral development. Gilligan addressed the fact that most women scored lower on Kohlberg's moral scales by proposing women were more influenced morally by interpersonal relationships and ethics of care responsibilities than by institutional rules and ethics of legal rights. After some initial reservations, in time Kohlberg came to see Gilligan's point of view and joined her to develop a descriptive ethics of conduct in relationships. They referred to this effort as the "just community" or "ethical community." Kohlberg viewed this community of practice as one having a core global network of knowledgeable experts, i.e., an epistemic community, whose authority others trusted for promoting moral growth in children, adult prisoners, etc., and for resolving conflicts. With Gilligan and Kohlberg each representing their different respective approaches to moral development, they participated in "democratic educational interventions" as part of the ethical community project. These interventions remain the standard of measurement in ethical relationship psychology.

Gilligan's *In a Different Voice* was a feminist response to Kohlberg's original theory of moral development, which she found male-oriented to the exclusion of female concerns. Like other traditional ethics developed by and oriented to male perceptions, behaviors, and issues, most of Kohlberg's theory focused on laws and rules rather than relationships. Children in his Pre-Conventional-Level first stage behaved obediently to avoid punishment; in the Pre-Conventional second stage, their behavior was instrumentally determined for achieving their purposes. Only his Conventional-level third stage, the Morality of Interpersonal Cooperation or "Good Boy-Nice Girl" stage involved interactions among individuals. His Conventional-Level fourth "Law and Order" stage returned to laws, focusing on maintaining the social order. Kohlberg's Post-Conventional fifth stage again concerned laws and social contracts, albeit at a more abstract level; and his Post-Conventional sixth stage, the Universal Ethical Principle, while legal autonomy transcended legal obedience, law was still central. Contrastingly, Gilligan asserted that relationships rather than rules governed female ethics, explaining why women appeared lower on Kohlberg's moral scales: because they responded morally more to interpersonal dynamics of care than legal principles of right.

Relationship ethics applied to traditional ethics

Lawrence Kohlberg's theory of moral development, structurally based on Piaget's theory of cognitive development, focused on traditional ethical concepts of rules, laws, and rights. Only one of the six stages he formulated made explicit reference to interpersonal relationships as its basis; the others were primarily concerned with instrumental, contractual and legal orientations and universal ethical principles. Carol Gilligan then proposed that women scored lower on Kohlberg's moral measures not by being less morally developed, but because their moral development was relational, not legal, influenced by care and responsibilities more than laws and rights. Kohlberg's and Gilligan's theories influenced each other: while evincing divergent approaches, they agreed on many things, collaborating on the original just community project. This history informs Kohlberg's continuing interest in relationships, influencing others: his student Burton Visotzky (*The Genesis of Ethics,* 1997) applied this relationship orientation to Biblical ethics, explaining personal choices and interpersonal interactions of main characters in the book of Genesis. Referring to the Talmud and Midrash, he shows ethical relationships were frequently central to Jewish theological traditions—relationships among family, community, or tribal members as well as between God and humans.

Philosophers who devoted attention to relational ethics

Mohandas Gandhi's ethical thought contained diverse influences. Among these, he was influenced by the Jain religion, which teaches principles of compassion and not harming any other living being. Gandhi applied these to his own ideas of using only nonviolent protest and resistance for effecting social reform, and of addressing other human interactions compassionately and nonviolently. While influenced by Plato, who saw absolute ideals as truths superior to relative, transitory human realities he deemed illusory, Gandhi nonetheless theorized absolute reality can only be understood relatively in the context of human interactions and events. Confucius's philosophy emphasized sincerity and correctness in social interactions, including family loyalty and respect; he advocated ideal government based on family, and early instances of the Golden and Silver Rules. Empathy and understanding for others were foundational virtues of Confucius's moral system. Baruch Spinoza, while a rationalist, believed in the human relativity of good and evil. Similarly to Gandhi, he taught a "philosophy of tolerance and benevolence." The contemporary New Confucian and Green philosophies also include relational traditions among their significant influences.

Business relationships

Research into human interactions in the context of business relationships has included studies of the relative congruence between individual employees and their employing organizations. Such investigations of "person-organization fit" include examinations of value congruence. Further, some studies (cf. Shen and Kim, 2012) examine person-organization fit in terms of ethical values specifically. These researchers define ethics as principles or rules applied for solving problems where values and morals are at issue. They define morals as traditions in beliefs about behaviors that are right and wrong, which have evolved over long periods of time. They define values as beliefs concerning which concepts or things are important. Furthermore, although they note that public relations researchers have not yet investigated relationships between person-organization ethical fit to organization-public interactions, they speculate that perceptions of ethical person-organization fit can serve as one "source of tension" affecting the relationship between an organization and its "employee public." Organizational psychology research finds person-organization fit contributes to higher employee satisfaction and commitment. Researchers find effective communication strategies enhance person-organization fit on ethical values.

Sexual ethics

Following St. Thomas Aquinas, the Natural Law approach to sexual morality finds human behavior must adhere to a God-given order, dictating a code of sexual ethics that is more restrictive. In contrast, the secular liberal ethical perspective rejects the idea that unnatural sexual acts are not necessarily immoral, emphasizing self-determination, free choice, and pleasure for informing moral judgments regarding sexual behavior. Secular liberal philosophers identify rape as the paramount example of a sexual act that is always morally wrong, owing to its coercive character. Manipulative or dishonest sexual actions are also considered morally wrong by secular liberals. Voluntary, consensual sexual activities, however, are typically acceptable morally in the liberal view. Natural law theorists agree that coercive, manipulative, or dishonest sexual actions are morally wrong, but believe unnatural acts are also morally wrong independently. For example, Kant found both homosexual sex and masturbation morally wrong by being unnatural, while secular liberals do not.

Proponents of Natural Law in the tradition of St. Thomas Aquinas believe that, during casual sex, even though it is truly consensual, people are simply using one another for sexual pleasure and thus are engaging in sexual activity that is not virtuous. For example, Immanuel Kant and Pope John Paul II (born Karol Wojtyla) both believed that people made objects of themselves by willingly permitting themselves to be used sexually. Kant found in his *Lectures* (1750s-1790s) that only within marriage did people avoid treating and being treated as means to an end, because in marriage, both partners attained a kind of metaphysical unity through surrendering physically and spiritually to one another. In *Love and Responsibility* (1960 Polish, 1981 English), Wojtyla stated, "only love can preclude the use of one person by another" because love unifies individuals through the reciprocal gifts of their selves to one another. Theologians Patricia Jung and Ralph Smith (*Heterosexism*, 1993) thus argue that monogamous, loving homosexual/lesbian marriages would morally justify homosexual/lesbian sexual activity. Natural Law proponents reject homosexual marriage when defining sexual activity as only permissible within marriage.

In sexual ethics, one debate concerns whether consensual sexual activity is sufficient to meet the requirements for morality when no harm to any third party is involved. Ethical philosophers subscribing to the tradition of Natural Law find that consent is not enough because they believe it is morally wrong to engage in unnatural sexual acts, even when both participants do so willingly. In addition to Natural Law proponents, moral perfectionists and moral paternalists would likewise find it morally wrong to engage in consensual sexual activity in the case of activity that becomes harmful. Harming another and/or allowing another to harm oneself are judged morally wrong even when consensual; consent is not sufficient in such cases, which would include some instances of sadomasochism. Philosophers who believe sexual activity is only acceptable within a committed relationship also often presume consent is insufficient. They view sexual activity as justified morally only when accompanied by marriage, love, devotion, etc.; without some such commitment, the activity constitutes objectifying or using one or both participants, which they find morally unacceptable.

In "Sexual Morality and the Concept of Using Another Person" (2002), Thomas A. Mappes finds voluntary, consensual sexual activity, absent harm to third parties, morally acceptable: "respect for persons entails that each of us recognize the rightful authority of other persons (as rational beings) to conduct their individual lives as they see fit." Others (cf. Soble) remark that observing another's consent respects his or her capacities for autonomous reasoning and choosing, whereas not permitting another's consent is paternalistic and disrespectful. This position precludes moral prohibitions against casual sex, promiscuity, or sex with strangers provided these are truly consensual. However, they also note the need to answer certain questions regarding Mappes' criterion of free and informed consent: how specific consent must be, e.g., which types of sexual activities; and how explicit consent must be, e.g., verbal, nonverbal, involuntary, etc. Some philosophers maintain consent requires extreme specificity and only explicit, verbal communication.

Some philosophers, e.g., Thomas A. Mappes and others, define voluntary, informed consent as the criterion for sexual activity to be morally acceptable. However, other philosophers do not necessarily agree that consent always must be completely voluntary for sexual activity to be morally permitted. For example, Jeffrie Murphy ("Some Ruminations on Women, Violence, and the Criminal Law," 1998), find certain "threats," e.g., "Have sex with me or I will find another girlfriend"; and offers, e.g., "Have sex with me and I will marry you" to be "morally permissible": "We negotiate our way through most of life with schemes of threats and offers," and he sees no reason to exclude sexuality. With threats, the implication is that they can be coercive, which would make one person's participation in the activity less than voluntary; yet Murphy finds such threats are not always wrong morally. On the other hand, it can be argued (cf. Wertheimer, "Consent and Sexual Relations", 2009) that when one person makes threats or offers, the other is still free to refuse or participate voluntarily. This argument would negate Murphy's contention that sexual activity can be morally correct without always involving voluntary consent.

Poverty and economic inequality

The poverty head count, the Gini index of inequality, and similar indicators using statistical values and approaching their subjects from a pragmatic perspective represent the historical foundations of the study of poverty and inequality indices. Recent research has revealed that inequality indices can be afforded ethical content that is more accessible by relating them to functions of social welfare. Rather than only assessing distribution in a descriptive manner, an inequality index would be more meaningful if it also assessed the damage that inequality does to social welfare. Kolm (1969) has provided a simple method for using a social welfare function for deriving an inequality index, which was then made more popular by Atkinson (1970) and Sen (1973). This involves a symmetrical social welfare function defined by income distributions: permutations of two individuals' incomes do not change social welfare. Wherever income is distributed unequally, an equal distribution yielding the same social welfare can be computed. This is named the "equal-equivalent" or "equally-distributed equivalent" distribution.

Although some economists do not consider the ethics of distributive justice a part of economics, others as well as ethicists and other philosophers observe that economics includes a significant body of literature devoted to economic and social justice and associated normative issues. Insights to these can be derived from various economic approaches and theories, including the theory of inequality and poverty measurement. Compared to other topics in economics and ethics, this theory has developed relatively recently. Since its inception, several economists have published outstanding surveys of it between 1989 and 2002, including Lambert (1989), Sen and Foster (1997), Silber (1999), Cowell (2000), Dutta (2002), and Chakravarty (1990 and 2009). Despite its relative recency, this theory bears initial consideration because it bases evaluating social circumstances in the context of clearly assessed personal status, which has the greatest simplicity and lends itself to a variety of comparisons among individuals. Whereas normative economics otherwise acknowledges the multiple dimensions of individual well-being, largely wrestling with their resistance to synthesis within one measure, this theory is the exception for its traditional focus on income inequality and the accompanying, more positive assumption of clearly defined measurement of individual well-being.

Creating an inequality index

Calculating an egalitarian distribution of income between any two individuals that would produce the same social welfare as an unequal distribution of income is known as the equal-equivalent or equally-distributed equivalent distribution method (Kolm, 1969). This method makes the social welfare function averse to inequality. This equality causes the total income amount in the equal-equivalent distribution to be less than it was in the unequal distribution. This means that the social welfare function allows some of the total income to be sacrificed as a means of achieving equality. Measuring this loss of income in proportion to the original total income can perform as a useful inequality index. Reciprocally, this index of income inequality can also be applied to deconstruct social welfare in a pictorial manner. Given a constant population, one minus the inequality index, multiplied by the average income or total income, gives an ordinally equivalent measure of social welfare.

The method (Kolm, 1969) of using the equal-equivalent distribution to formulate an index of inequality informed by a social welfare function is commonly known as the "ethical approach" to the measurement of inequality. The social welfare function used is symmetrical, i.e., not changed by permutations of two individual incomes, and defined by individual income distributions. If two people's incomes are different, one computes how their total income would be distributed equally to result in the same social welfare in which the original, unequal distribution resulted. This equal-equivalent distribution removes some of the total income in exchange for conferring equality to the social welfare function. The ratio of the decrease in income to the original total income provides an inequality index, as well as one of equivalent social welfare. This ethical approach to inequality measurement is best applied in cases when the distribution of individual well-being (measured according to income or otherwise) is the purpose of measuring inequality and the defense of the social welfare function. The underlying ethical principles of the social welfare function are hence reflected by its egalitarian, symmetrical, and impartial character.

Instance wherein the ethical approach to inequality measurement is not best applied

The ethical approach to inequality measurement constructs an inequality index informed by a social welfare function by calculating the equal-equivalent distribution, wherein two unequal individual incomes are recalculated to be equal such that they would still produce the same social welfare as when they were unequal. In the process, some total income is subtracted to achieve equality. This subtracted amount relative to the original total income gives an inequality index. Total or average income (given a fixed population) multiplied by one minus that inequality index gives a numerical equivalent social welfare measure. This approach is best applied when inequality is measured for the purposes of distribution of individual well-being and support of the social welfare function. However, when social welfare is dependent on individual well-being, and individual well-being in turn is dependent on income—with some individual differences based on different needs—this approach is less applicable: because needier individuals could need more income than others, income equality becomes less appropriate as a goal.

Cases in which the ethical approach to measuring inequality is indicated and contraindicated

The ethical approach, i.e., deriving an inequality index using a social welfare function, is most applicable in cases when upholding the social welfare function and distributing individual welfare equally are the goals. However, cases when income determines individual well-being, which determines social welfare, and income equality is not ideal in cases of differential need, the ethical approach is less indicated; it can be used to produce an index of inequality in well-being, but not in income. In such cases, income inequality is not necessarily undesirable, e.g., when addressing differential need. Applying the ethical approach, though inappropriate, would illuminate this. The ethical approach would be interpreted differently when the utilitarian sum of all individual utilities comprises the social welfare, and all individuals have the same utility function, a strictly concave one—i.e., having a descending marginal utility. In this case, the inequality index lacks the ethical principle of avoiding social welfare function inequality: the social welfare function is not averse to inequality in utilities. It simply shows the outcome of empirical evidence regarding how concave individual utility functions are. In this context, the ethical approach is not really ethical.

Formulating ethical axioms by recent researchers into indices of economic inequality

Recent research into indices of inequality has yielded an alternative ethical approach that entails studying the properties of indices by formulating and applying axioms. The primary ethical axioms involve transfers. For example, the Pigou-Dalton principle of transfers states that social welfare increases, or inequality decreases, when a wealthier and poorer individual make an even transfer without reversal of their ranks within the pair (regardless of whether their ranking among other individuals is changed). The weakness of this axiom is that the condition requires even transfers. Accordingly, researchers have proposed additional axioms to give those at a disadvantage a stronger priority. According to Kolm's (1976) principle of diminishing transfers, the lower in a distribution a Pigou-Dalton transfer occurs, the greater its impact is. Fleurbaey and Michel's (2001) principle of proportional transfers states that, when a donor gives and a beneficiary receives amounts proportionate to their original positions, this inefficient transfer augments social welfare.

Ethical axiom of economic transfer that has been developed to apply to measures of poverty

Recent research into indices of economic inequality has applied ethical axioms to study the characteristics of the indices. For example, even transfers between richer and poorer individuals lower inequality and raise social welfare; as a corollary, this principle has greater impact the lower it is in a distribution, and social welfare increases when giving and receiving are proportionate to both parties' original positions. Analogously to these axioms regarding inequality, Sen proposed an axiom regarding poverty (1976) that, when an even transfer occurs between somebody with income below the poverty line and somebody with income—whether below or above the poverty line—is higher than the first person's, poverty increases. This is the converse of the axioms stating conditions under which social welfare increases. Other axioms used to analyze economic inequality and poverty are less overtly ethical in nature, typically deal with scale invariance, index decomposability, etc. Researchers have produced characterization results identifying categories of indices that meet specific groups of axioms. Both ethical approaches can be combined by making the condition axiomatic that an index is derived from a social welfare function with specific characteristics.

Problem in the measurement of inequality and poverty related to the availability of indice

Even with axioms defining specific subcategories, indices of inequality and poverty remain so numerous that they present a significant application problem of determining the relative inequality or poverty of any distribution in that the number of indices for reference is unlimited. This problem, while ostensibly practical in nature, has nonetheless generated findings both deep in character and broad in scope. These offer a relationship among the use of poverty and inequality indices to address transfer axioms, the overall characteristics of social welfare functions, and stochastic dominance as a statistical concept. This dominance approach to the empirical study of inequality is especially amenable to applying Lorenz curves showing what percent the poorest in a population have of a total amount measured, i.e., well-being, income, or wealth. The Census Bureau, for example, reported the poorest 20 percent of the population in 2006 had 3.7 percent of total income; the poorest 40 percent, 13.1 percent; the poorest 60 percent, 28.1; the poorest 80 percent, 50.6; and the top five percent of the population had 22.2 percent of total income. These proportions can be graphed with a Lorenz curve covering their points between zero and 100 percent. The curve contrasts from a straight diagonal representing a "perfect equality" line of equal distribution; the area between the two represents inequality.

Philosophical interest in the measurement of economic inequality

Since the 1990s, philosophy has taken an increasing interest in measuring inequality. However, most research focuses on definitions of the best bases for averting inequality. For example, some have proposed (cf. Parfit, 1995) prioritizing the poorer not owing to their position relative to the wealthier, but due to their being poor and how poor. Philosophers find this likely consistent with applying a social welfare function that can be additively separated, with decreasing marginal social utility, to define social welfare. When a social welfare function equals the sum of separate terms, each dependent on only one person's well-being, it is additively separable. This "priority" approach denies relative/comparative positions, which can be considered opposite to egalitarianism when egalitarianism is defined as dependent on comparative positions. If so, then a separable social welfare function cannot accurately represent egalitarian values. Ethically, then, separability of social welfare functions or decomposability of indices become more significant properties rather than simply convenient economics conditions to simplify functional forms.

Lorenz curves and what they represent visually in terms of social equality variables

In the first image (www.maxi-pedia.com), the straight diagonal line represents perfectly equal distribution, the ideal of perfect equality in income/wealth/well-being—whatever quantity is measured. The Lorenz curve to its right represents percentage points. The space between the equal distribution line and the Lorenz curve is referred to as the area of inequality, i.e., the difference between ideal and real. In the second image (https://ib-economics.wikispaces.com), the Lorenz curve is displayed without the perfect equality referent. Lorenz curves may be plotted with percentage of income/wealth/well-being along the vertical axis and population percentages along the horizontal, as in the first figure; or vice versa, i.e., population vertically and income/other quantity horizontally. Separate curves can also show income before/after taxes, benefits, etc.

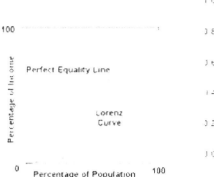
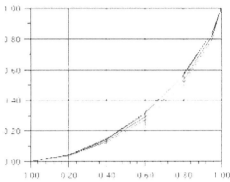

Egalitarian vs. prioritarian approaches

Ethicists, other philosophers, and economists (e.g., Tungodden 2003, Holtug and Lippert-Rasmussen 2007, among many) continue to debate the importance and substance of distinguishing between egalitarianism and prioritarianism. Additionally, a difference between economists and philosophers is that economists usually interpret inequality or social welfare strictly by social positions that are ranked ordinally, whereas philosophers more frequently consider social welfare/good or inequality as numerical quantities that are meaningful cardinally. Three perspectives for viewing equality, inequality, poverty, and social welfare are the egalitarian position, the prioritarian position, and the sufficiency position. The egalitarian view can be said to rest on the differences observed through comparing the relative positions of poorer and wealthier people. The prioritarian view, however, maintains that poorer people should be given priority not based on their position relative to wealthier people, but on their poverty and degree of it in itself. Prioritarianism would use an additively separable social welfare function to define social welfare, which would not apply to egalitarianism as it requires relativity. The sufficiency view proposes prioritizing only people with incomes beneath a given threshold. This view suggests social welfare may be summed up through poverty indices.

Welfare economics

Traditionally, the term "welfare economics" was a general name for normative economics (as opposed to positive economics). However, more recently, a number of theorists have proposed a "new" definition of welfare economics. Whereas welfare economics originally judged social welfare based on comparing utility interpersonally, today this term is more often associated with a narrower, specific subcategory of normative economics. Scholars attribute this shift possibly to the development of the social choice theory and other approaches similarly encompassing wider territory, and to the development of approaches described as "non-welfarist." Previously, without comparing individuals, welfare could only be judged by the Pareto principle that a global improvement benefits or does not harm every member of a given population. Variations on this principle involve the definition of individual improvement, and whether or not all individuals experience it. But the Pareto principle typically offers no insight regarding changes wrought by public policy, which usually benefit some groups at the expense of others. 20th-century authors have hence proposed other assessment methods.

The Pareto principle defining global improvement as benefiting/not harming each member of the population involved does not apply well to social changes stemming from public policy, which typically vary between helping and harming different sectors of the population. Therefore, some 20th-century authors proposed extending this principle via testing compensation. For example, one criterion (Kaldor, 1939) for global improvement is if those gaining could compensate those losing from the change after the fact. Another (Hicks, 1939) is if the former criterion did not apply, those losing could not compensate those gaining before the fact, in which case the opposite change in situations from A to B would be approved if the former criterion did not approve the change from B to A. While these criteria are not as partial as the Pareto criterion, there are still many pairs of alternatives they do not rank. Yet critics identify two more major problems: (1) in calculating compensation transfers, they can yield inconsistent social judgments (e.g., one A or B is superior to another B or A, and vice versa); and (2) such compensation tests are of questionable value ethically.

Because public policies inevitably are positive for some subgroups of a population and negative for others, the Pareto principle defining global improvement as either benefiting everybody or harming nobody is not useful. Thus some authors (cf. Kaldor, 1939 and Hicks, 1939) have proposed compensation tests related to transfers between those who benefited and those who suffered from policy changes. Critics have found, however, that social judgments based on such tests have two main problems. First, the same criterion can identify one type of situation A as better than another type of situation B, and vice versa. One author (Scitovsky, 1941) then suggested combining the two criteria proposed for compensation tests; however, this would still not preclude social judgments that were intransitive (e.g., if one held between A and B and between B and C, it would not hold between A and C). Second, in the first criterion (Kaldor), if those who gained could then compensate those who lost, everybody would gain and the Pareto principle alone would apply sufficiently. In the second criterion (Hicks), if compensation transfers do not occur, losers never gain, biasing the criterion toward the wealthy, limiting ethical value.

Among a number of variations that have developed in welfare economics, one subcategory that has emerged concentrates on the potential of using national income as a criterion for making social welfare judgments. While improved social welfare in a nation can be associated with improved national income there, strict assumptions are required for this to be accurate. The most obvious of these is the assumption that the nation under discussion has socially optimum income distribution. While this finding is quite restrictive, it has enduring influence on international economics theoretically, and on the significance of gross domestic product (GDP) growth in policy discussions practically. However, this influence on welfare economics of using national income as an indicator has also been resisted by another school of economic thought, which focuses on other social indicators instead. For example, economic well-being, social health, genuine progress, happiness, and other factors have been viewed as indices of social welfare. In recent years, the number of such social indicators has skyrocketed; cf. Miringoff and Miringoff, 1999; Frey and Stutzer, 2002; Kahneman et al., 2004; Gadrey and Jany-Catrice, 2006; and the journal, *Social Indicators Research,* for example.

Judging public influences on social economic welfare

Compensation tests have been proposed as alternatives to the Pareto principle for social evaluation when, as with public policies, variable social welfare occurs, obviating the Pareto criterion that every individual benefits or is unharmed as global improvement. Compensation tests are biased in favor of the wealthy because they are typically able and willing to pay highly for what they want to obtain, hence able to compensate losers with ease, and get to keep everything if they do not compensate them. Summation of willingness to pay across a population is the basis for similar criteria developed through cost-benefit analysis. Its practitioners, plus international economics, industrial organization and similar economic theories continue to utilize these criteria. Some theorists have produced more advanced variations of cost-benefit analysis, which address criticisms of its criteria's resulting in intransitive social judgments and being limited in ethical value due to bias, by depending on consistent social welfare functions or on weighing of the sums of willingness to pay. Many public economics specialists have discounted all inefficiency stemming from public policies and social organizations, maintaining that the Pareto principle is the essential ethical criterion for economists to use as support for social evaluations.

Bergson-Samuelson social welfare function

Bergson (1938) and Samuelson (1947, 1981) have incorporated, from old welfare economics, the aim of using clearly defined social welfare functions to assist producing consistent, complete social welfare judgments; and from new welfare economics, the concept that information included about individual preferences should be only that which is non-comparable and ordinal. Often called the Bergson-Samuelson social welfare function, is the formula: $W(U_1(x),...,U_n(x))$ where i = the individual, x = the social state, and $U_i(x)$, for i = 1,...n, is the individual (i)'s utility in the social state. The new social welfare concept of only retaining ordinal information about individual preferences appears to contradict this formula, which includes functions of individual utility. Various authors (cf. Arrow, 1951; Kemp and Ng, 1976; Samuelson 1977, 1987; Sen, 1986; and Fleurbaey and Mongin, 2005) have debated the potential of creating a Bergson-Samuelson social welfare function based solely upon non-comparable, ordinal, individual preferences. While many find Samuelson and his supporters have lost this debate, others contend they have been misunderstood.

Some welfare economy ethicists have argued that the Bergson-Samuelson social welfare function, combining elements of old and new welfare economics, is contradictory to their incorporated new social welfare concept of using only non-comparable, ordinal individual preference information because individual utility functions are included in their formula. Various authors have debated this issue, with Samuelson and his supporters appearing to be refuted by others. However, some economists observe this was a basic misunderstanding of the Bergson-Samuelson welfare function. Bergson and Samuelson themselves indicate that, based on principles of fairness, individual utility functions in their formula should be created from individual preference rankings. Samuelson (1977) and others (cf. Mayston, 1974; Pazner, 1979; and Mayston, 1982) have proven multiple times that constructing these functions is possible. No argument is found against the sufficiency of non-comparable, ordinal information alone for such a construction. Bergson and Samuelson have also conceded that interpersonal comparisons were necessary, but found these could be performed based only on non-comparable preference rankings and still be ethically pertinent. To criticisms about their lack of specificity regarding which fairness principles should justify this construction, some scholars (cf. Fleurbaey, 2012) suggest referring to the theory of fair allocation (cf. Kolm, 1972).

Race

Because over time, efforts to define racial groups and their boundaries have been beset by confusion and ambiguity, consensus has developed among many philosophers and other scholars that essential or distinct races are more socially constructed than biologically distinct. At the same time, though, controversy continues concerning whether contemporary anti-miscegenation practices and/or human evolution have produced enough genetic separation to warrant describing non-discrete groups of humans with common phenotypes and genotype clusters as races. Additional controversy concerns the development and nature of discrete, socially constructed racial classifications. Some find social hierarchies necessary to conceiving of race, while others believe in the possibility of egalitarian race relations. The moral status of racial identity and solidarity and the validity and justness of institutions and/or policies that intend to mitigate racial inequality are also topics of significant debate. One area of moral, political, and legal philosophy relevant to race examines its moral status. The other evaluates normatively particular institutions or policies like affirmative action aiming to rectify racial inequality. Both require reflecting on the metaphysics of race, but only the former addresses it consistently. Hence policies like affirmative action are debated without considering racial groups' ontological status.

Lawrence Blum, who sees race as socially constructed rather than biologically inherited, prefers the term "racialized group" to "race." He understands the necessity of social policies like affirmative action for rectifying racism and the harm it does, but he also questions their morality. Similarly, Anthony Appiah is opposed to the idea of races but in favor of the idea of racial identities. While he approves of racial identity as a basis for opposing racism, at the same time he warns that racial identities within groups can restrict their freedom when they conform to racial/cultural stereotypes themselves. To address both these authors' ambivalent attitudes, philosopher Tommie Shelby applies the Black Nationalism of Martin Delany. Shelby differentiates classical Black Nationalism, based on organic black identity, with pragmatic black nationalism, based on an instrumentalist position of overcoming racism against black people. The pragmatic nationalism enables black solidarity across culture and class, based on commitment to principles of justice and racial equality as well as common interests. Hence solidarity lies not in shared identity but principled response to shared oppression. This rationalism avoids the biological orientation to race that Blum disapproves of, and the dangers of cultural conformity that Appiah attributes to racial identity.

Racism

Lawrence Blum (2002) refers to two factors defining racism: (1) inferiorization, i.e., denigrating a racial group on the basis of some supposed biological inferiority; and (2) antipathy, i.e., hostility, hatred, and bigotry against a racial group on the basis of its supposed hereditary physical characteristics. Blum finds these moral sins deserving of being condemned by the term "racism" owing to their violation of norms for dignity, equality, and respect; and to their historical association with overt, extreme instances of racial oppression. However, because "racism" becomes a very morally charged word due to these associations, Blum finds it should not be used to describe "lesser racial ills and infractions" which appear to be the results of simpler instances of discomfort, ignorance, or insensitivity related to members of other racial groups. He points out that labeling these latter types of less serious racial offenses would judge the people responsible disproportionately, which would prohibit engaging them in productive moral dialogues that could edify and ultimately rectify their attitudes and behaviors.

Blum (2002) cites the historical association of severe oppression with racism to support his contention that the term "race" should not be used. He also objects to this term because he does not find clear biological grounds for it. He recommends instead using the phrase "racialized group" to identify group identities sharing common physical characteristics. To Blum, these common characteristics are supposed by many to be inherited, but the identities based on them are constructed socially. He finds the term "racialized group" distances the concept of race from biological origins, and also allows degrees rather than absolutes. For example, Blum describes Latinos as an "incompletely racialized group" where such degrees apply. Blum sees no conflict between such a shift in terminology emphasizing sociological construction of identities and policies like affirmative action that are specific to racial groups. Even if their racialized identities are socially constructed, members of such groups still sustain true harm. To redress such harm, laws may need to identify individuals by racialized identities. However, Blum also expresses ambivalence regarding these policies, finding them morally suspect despite being necessary.

Just as Blum expresses ambivalence toward affirmative action and similar policies, seeing them as both realistically necessary and morally suspect; and views race as more socially constructed than biologically determined, Appiah also expresses ambivalence on these topics. Metaphysically, he bases his "eliminative" normative perspective on his sense of racial skepticism, similar to Blum's. Appiah has written (1996) that he is "for racial identities," though "against races." He realizes that, due to the widespread social consensus about the existence of races, individual people are assigned to races notwithstanding their personal wishes or choices. Further, compared to ethnic identity, Appiah identifies racial identity as much more significant and costly to people. Hence he finds racially related mobilization warranted for fighting racism. Yet he also expresses caution about "scripts" or cultural norms that have attained dominance in certain racial groups, which by dictating the behaviors of their members, can limit individual autonomy. Therefore, Appiah's conclusion is, "Racial identity can be the basis of resistance to racism; but even as we struggle against racism... let us not let our racial identities subject us to new tyrannies."

Policies that practical philosophy related to race has addressed

Practical philosophers concerned with the subject of race have written about such public policies as affirmative action, color-blindness in laws and policies, and race-conscious electoral districting. The vast body of literature concerning affirmative action can be classified into four types of approaches: those that emphasize compensatory justice, those that emphasize distributive justice, those that critique the idea of merit, and those that focus on diversity among perspectives. For example, Alan Goldman (1979) has opposed the idea of affirmative action on the basis of the principle that educational and occupational opportunities should be awarded to the most qualified individuals rather than members of specified racial groups. He states that race is an irrelevant factor, excepting in cases when specific individuals have been discriminated against racially or otherwise—in which case race may be considered in awarding compensatory opportunities. Ronald Fiscus (1992) argues in favor of distributive justice rather than compensation. He argues that, without a racist society's influences, educational and occupational success would be randomly distributed across races, hence distributive justice demands distributing university admissions and jobs with racial proportionality.

Race-conscious electoral districting and descriptive racial representation

Race-conscious electoral districting is the practice of defining the geographical boundaries of electoral districts in such a way that members of a racial minority group become the majority of voters in one district. Descriptive racial representation is the practice of electing officials to represent electoral districts on the basis of the premise that members of different racial groups will receive the best representation by politicians who are also members of their racial group. One example of a way in which the practices of race-conscious electoral districting and descriptive racial representation are related is that districts where the majority of constituents are black are far more likely to elect representatives who are also black. But at the same time, these two practices are not necessarily connected, as evidenced by the fact that districts with majority black constituencies also frequently elect white representatives (James, 2011). James also refers to an "early, though critical discussion of the problem of descriptive representation" by Pitkin (1967).

Participants in discussions of political philosophy about descriptive racial representation

Iris Young (1990) has defended descriptive representation for racial minorities and for women, based on both having experienced oppression and domination, which she finds institutionally limits their self-determination. Extending this argument, Anne Phillips (1995) has proposed legislative deliberation can be improved by racial minority representatives. Melissa Williams (1998) has also defended descriptive racial representation for its contribution to legislative deliberation, additionally pointing out that, because both minority constituents and representatives will be affected by laws covertly or overtly discriminating against them, minority constituents are more likely to trust minority representatives. Jane Mansbridge (1999) has reasoned that, to demonstrate the internal diversity within minority groups, as well as to advocate sufficiently for the shared interests of minority groups, enough elected minority representatives must attain a "critical mass." To criticisms that descriptive representation indicates group essentialism because not all racial group members have common opinions or interests, Young (2000) later responded that members of a racial group do indeed share common experiences informing a common "social perspective"; though others (James, 2011) have disagreed.

Affirmative action

A basic definition of affirmative action is actions that are positively made to compensate for the historical exclusion of minority groups, including women, from equal representation in cultural, educational, and employment domains by augmenting the proportions of these groups that are represented. Affirmative action becomes controversial when the actions taken to increase minority representation entail selecting members of minority groups based on their race, ethnicity, gender or other minority status—i.e., selecting them preferentially. Such controversial preferential selection of minority group members, and its opposition and defense, have developed following two courses. One course is through public discussion, which has generated an immense body of literature both opposing and defending preferential affirmative action. The other course is through administrative and legal avenues, wherein the executive, legislative, and judicial branches of government have enacted and implemented laws and rules mandating affirmative action. An inherent problem is that these two courses have not interacted sufficiently, so public controversies often lack legal support.

Ronald Fiscus (1992) finds distributive justice dictates distributing educational and occupational opportunities in a racially proportionate manner, consistent with how they would be randomly distributed if the influence of a racist society were eliminated. One way this differs from arguments that merit should decide school and job opportunities rather than race, opposing affirmative action policies (cf. Goldman, 1979) is that distribution of admissions and jobs in proportion to racial distribution negates considering merit in admission and job offers (James, 2011). However, Iris Young (1970) has countered that pre-college secondary school achievement, standardized test scores, and similar contemporary measures used as criteria of merit are inherently biased against socially disadvantaged racial and other groups. Moreover, she notes these seldom have much functional relation to higher academic or workplace potential. Alternatively, to substantive justice theories concerning how goods are awarded, Jürgen Habermas (1990) defines justice as a fair procedure of discourse without power relations or coercion, considering all pertinent views. Influenced by Habermas, Michel Rosenfeld (1991) favors a reversibility concept of justice, defending affirmative action as a way to incorporate racially diverse perspectives.

Scholars observe that historically, public discussion about affirmative action can be visualized as having two major peaks over the past several decades. The first surge in controversy started in approximately 1972 and continued until it declined following 1980. This debate was focused mainly on preferential treatment based on both race and gender equally. In this early period, affirmative action was equally concerned not only with higher education settings, but also equally with workplace settings, including both blue-collar and white-collar work environments. This concern explains the dual attention to race and gender of the debate. The second peak in controversy over affirmative action took place in the 1990s and culminated in 2003, when the Supreme Court ruled to uphold specific types of affirmative action. This debate was more exclusively focused on race and ethnicity and concerned primarily with college admissions. The reason for this focus is that around the turn of the 21st century, women did not need the support that African-American and Hispanic students did to gain admission to selective colleges and universities.

The Civil Rights Act of 1964 first stipulated affirmative action as recourse for federal courts against those violating this law. In 1965, President Lyndon B. Johnson issued Executive Order 11246, requiring affirmative action by federal contractors to prevent/correct discrimination. However, this order delegated formulating rules to implement it to the Secretary of Labor. Meanwhile, federal courts enforced the Civil Rights Act to correct discrimination by unions, employers, and others; and the Department of Labor implemented an ad-hoc assault on the building industry by negotiating, threatening, coaxing, bullying, and otherwise manipulating resistant construction companies to comply with regional plans wherein they had to commit to targeted hiring numbers. The Labor Department used these contractors' agreements as indirect routes for pressuring labor unions providing workers to job sites. The Department of Health, Education, and Welfare's (HEW) 1970 Order No. 4 mandated universal goals, schedules, and "underutilization analyses" on all businesses contracting with the government, including universities. Though somewhat controversial, affirmative action had low public priority until 1972, when the Labor Secretary's revision of the 1970 order implemented it fully.

The US Department of Health, Education, and Welfare (HEW) had issued Order No. 4 in 1970 to impose affirmative action measures on all businesses with government contracts, including universities. Only in 1972 did the Secretary of Labor issue Revised Order No. 4, effectively implementing the earlier order. Initially, the administrations and faculties of universities, though bemused by the initial order's rules, experienced little threat to the status quo from it. At the time, annual numbers of PhDs awarded to racial and ethnic minorities were minuscule, limiting their qualification for teaching positions. Universities would have to search more diligently for minority recruits under the initial mandate to augment their representation; however, their efforts would still replicate historical patterns. In contrast, the 1972 Revised Order included women among minority "protected classes." More women were obtaining PhDs at far greater and more increasing rates than African-Americans and Hispanics. The "proportional representation" required by Revised Order No. 4 affected campuses more significantly due to including women. These new rules were met by equally strong campus reactions both for and against them.

During the same time period that 1972's HEW Revised Order No. 4 mandated increased university representation of "under-utilized" minorities including women, provoking heated controversy, Anglo-American philosophy experienced a "public turn." Philosophers had heretofore been viewed as capable of formulating meta-ethics analyzing justice concepts, but not normative ethics to recommend actual justice actions like social policies, political principles, or constitutional measures. But in the 1970s, two philosophical events overthrew this perception. First, John Rawls' *A Theory of Justice* (1971) defended a normative theory of justice with great eloquence and detail. Second, Florida State University founded the journal *Social Theory and Practice*; a few months later, Princeton University founded the journal *Philosophy & Public Affairs*. These publications, plus the remodeled existing journal *Ethics*, responded to the need philosophers felt to act rather than just talk about ethics in light of current events like the Vietnam War, Civil Rights Movement, and Women's Liberation Movement by providing new platforms for politically and socially engaged philosophical writing. For example, in 1973, "Equal Treatment and Compensatory Justice" by Thomas Nagel and "Preferential Hiring" by Judith Jarvis Thomson were published in *Philosophy & Public Affairs*.

After the Department of Health, Education, and Welfare (HEW) passed its Revised Order No. 4 in 1972, all entities contracting with the government, including higher education institutions, were mandated to increase their utilization of minority groups, including women, as "protected classes." Around the same time, a public shift in philosophy enabled ethicists to propose normative ethics rather than only meta-ethics, allowing them to become more directly and actively engaged in affirmative action measures instead of only discussing abstract concepts at a distance from social and political involvement. One issue they contested relative to Revised Order No. 4 was its requiring all contractors to meet goals and timetables: the question became whether such goals equaled quotas that would force employers to hire/admit preferentially regarding gender or race. Ethicists answering this question negatively found a correct interpretation of affirmative action would not allow preferential treatment. Those answering it positively found affirmative action would enable, if not require, preferences. Among this latter group, some found preferential hiring/admissions morally permissible; others did not.

The US Department of Health, Education, and Welfare (HEW)'s Revised Order No. 4 (1972) mandated affirmative action by all institutions contracting with the government, including hiring and admissions by universities. Ethicists debated the moral implications of these requirements. Even philosophers who agreed on defending preferential treatment disagreed on the reasons for it. For example, Thomson (1973) found preferential policies to achieve justice by redressing the historical exclusion from higher education and employment of African-Americans and women. But Nagel (1973) defended preferential treatment on the grounds of achieving social welfare without damaging justice. Their essays presenting these respective arguments were both published in the same journal (Princeton University's *Philosophy & Public Affairs*). Ethicists found that, for various reasons, it was appropriate for institutions to abandon previous standards of hiring/admitting based on merit, on the grounds that it was impossible to defend the entire system of basing financial rewards on credentials earned.

While some ethicists defended affirmative action (cf. Thomson, 1973; Nagel, 1973) on grounds of justice or social good, many critics (cf. Simon, 1974; Sher, 1975; Goldman, 1976; Sher, 1979) objected that viewing preferential hiring as redressing past wrongs appeared contradictory by helping women and African-Americans with good educational qualifications, who were least likely hurt by historical injustices; and harming white, younger male candidates who were least likely to have caused such injustices. Others also argued that preferential treatment, rather than effecting justice, violated the rights of applicants to equal consideration (Thomson, 1973; Simon, 1974); to open positions for those most competent (Goldman 1976, 1979); and/or to equal opportunity for everybody (Gross, 1977, 1978). Critics furthermore accused preferential policies of undermining the ability to reward individuals who deserved it based on their talents, characters, and choices (Simon, 1979) by making behavior and merit subordinate to race (Eastland and Bennett, 1979); and by separating true damages and liabilities from results (Gross, 1978).

Enforcing the Civil Rights Act in the workplace

Employers discarding segregating policies following the Civil Rights Act's passage could nonetheless continue existing, ostensibly neutral rules. For example, policies requiring employees transferring to another department to relinquish their seniority in the previous department would prevent advancement for older African-American maintenance staff just as much as former segregating rules prohibiting departmental transfers. Hence courts began overturning such "facially neutral" rules, separating discrimination from intent. The Supreme Court justified this via a 1971 interpretation of Title VII of the Civil Rights Act. Its identification of any unnecessary exclusion as statutory discrimination provided the background for forming a generic concept of affirmative action. Hiring quotas became stronger measures for temporarily correcting historical, ongoing, and future discrimination throughout the 1970s. A judicial dilemma that developed, unanticipated by Congress in passing the Civil Rights Act, was whether to require corrective racial preferences of resistant or incompetent defendants—violating Title VII's prohibition against racial preference; or require less objectionable but less effectual actions, enabling continuing discrimination—violating Title VII's provision for eliminating discrimination. The Court's resolution was to justify racial preferences as needed to prevent current and future discrimination.

Punishment

In the first half of the 20th century, punishment as a concept was defined, applied, and justified as a means of rehabilitating and reforming those who violated the laws. However, in the second half of the 20th century, this thinking shifted noticeably toward viewing punishment instead as a means of confining and exacting retribution against criminal offenders. Today, ethicists find that punishment is accepted as being intrinsically retributive in conception, regardless of what its further purposes might be. Liberal thinkers justify punishment based on the argument that, because expecting victims of criminal offenses to be responsible for the costs of crimes against them is unfair, and because the social order cannot be accomplished without punishment, the practice and the potential of punishment are needed by society. Due process of law and other controls over applying potential punishments are also necessitated by the human potential to abuse power and authority. Philosophers find both consequential and deontological ethical factors must be considered in justifying punishment.

In real-world politics, perceptions and interpretations of punishment have undergone developments that have mutually both affected and been affected by philosophical thinking about this topic. In the 1970s, criminologists, penologists, and sociologists alike lost faith in the effectiveness of prison programs intended to rehabilitate offenders, which failed to decrease recidivism. Consequently, they came to doubt the current penal philosophy would admit of the goal of rehabilitation as even feasible. Additionally, their skepticism extended to the effectiveness of using punishment as a deterrent, either as specific to each offender or general to the public. After eliminating these as purposes or effects of punishment, all that appeared to remain rationally were retribution and social defense. Advocates for public policy maintained that incapacitating convicted repeat offenders through imprisonment was the most economical means of decreasing crime; some even advocated the death penalty (cf. Wilson, 1975). Regardless of value judgments, in sheer numbers such proposed incarceration has been accomplished: by 2005, the US had over 2 million federal and state prisoners, including more than 3,700 on death row.

While prevailing attitudes in the latter half of the 20th century had left behind the aims of rehabilitating and reforming criminals in favor of incapacitating and confining them, policy analysts concurrently became disenchanted with prison sentences of indeterminate length. These had been necessary for allowing penal authorities the discretion to implement plans to promote rehabilitation. However, for determining policy, fairness became a consideration once rehabilitation and deterrence were becoming subordinate to retribution and incapacitation. By the 1980s, the most probable way to achieve justice when sentencing convicted criminals appeared to be determinate durations, not indeterminate ones (cf. Allen, 1981). However, theorists and policymakers additionally found that, even when defined, sentences still could only be fair if the offenders deserved the punishments assigned. By combining both concepts of justice and desert, they developed the doctrine of just deserts sentencing. Through this process, social theorists and politicians alike came to perceive incapacitation and retribution as more important goals than rehabilitation and deterrence; in some cases, the former entirely replaced the latter.

Police attacks on prisoners during the 1972 prison riots in Attica, New York represented a peak in penal officials' unhappiness with the system. This was reinforced by widespread social and legal developments like the concept of just deserts sentencing. At the same time, philosophers were developing ethical arguments that revived Hegel's and Kant's theories and were unexpectedly congruent with prevailing legal, penal, and social thinking. Firstly, philosophers argued punishment was not practiced for the purpose—primary or secondary—of reforming convicted criminals. An example cited (Bedau and Kelly, 2010) of such reform, particularly an extreme, medically based version, is in the fictional novel *A*

Clockwork Orange by Anthony Burgess (1962). Ethicists found such reformative punishment not only impractical, but also morally inadequate for both disrespecting offenders' autonomy and defying their "right" to punishment (Morris, 1968). Secondly, philosophers argued sentencing was responsible for just punishment; offender guilt and damage to the victim(s) and society determined sentencing justice (cf. Card, 1973; Nozick, 1981; von Hirsch, 1985). Hence retributive punishment was just. Philosophers found punishment unavoidably retributive by definition—both in theory as norms of justice in punishment, and in practice as the purposes of punishment.

One outcome of the shift from the middle 20th-century ideals, of rehabilitation and deterrence through imprisonment for indeterminate durations, to the later goals of retribution and incapacitation through imprisonment for determinate durations, was an end to the practice of releasing prisoners on parole. Another outcome was an increase in probation as an alternative to incarceration. In theory only, uniform determinate sentencing should replace release on parole. The purposes of uniformity were to assure equal justice for all offenders and incapacitate them; the purpose of determinate sentences was to avert unattainable goals for rehabilitation. However, these purposes were altered by political processes, as not all proponents of just punishment approved of determinate sentences. The Sentencing Reform Act of 1984, establishing the US Sentencing Commission and Federal Sentencing Guidelines, represented the peak of this process. The approach of just deserts sentencing has been criticized both theoretically and practically, and in most instances can be found irrational in practice; yet in the 21st century thus far, it has not been supplemented with any alternative philosophy.

In addition to two main trends in punishment—(1) the belief that punishment for reform of offenders is morally unacceptable as well as impractical, and (2) the belief that punishment for retribution of offenders is just—a third factor has not influenced penal policy as much, but has been equally significant theoretically: (3) a rethinking in the late 1980s of punitive practices stemming from Michel Foucault's writing in the mid-1970s about practices of punishment. Foucault had called attention to societal and political forces that mirror the types of power predominating in any given era, e.g., power for destruction, suppression, coercion, threat, or transformation, and presented the perception of legal punitive practices as subject to these social forces. In addition, regarding claims that society had rendered punishment more humane by substituting the covert containment of modern prison systems and buildings for the past's overt, uncontained, violent corporeal punishment, Foucault (1977) had expressed his profound skepticism.

The understandings of punishment that Foucault contributed were founded in his historical, psychodynamic, and socioeconomic perspectives. According to Foucault, the ideal of justice in punishment, the purposes claimed for punishment, and the norms controlling how power was used to seek those purposes all disguised other motivations, often unconscious, of reformers that contradicted their arguments of rationalism dating back to Enlightenment times. According to Foucault's theory, then, the late 18th century's movement opposing capital punishment could not be explained by the kind of rational, conscious utilitarian logic that Bentham and Beccaria had cited as influencing them (cf. Maestro, 1973; Bedau, 1983). Rather, Foucault found this movement was explained more by (1) the distaste Enlightenment intellectuals developed against the drama and theater of public executions; and (2) a "self-deceiving" (Bedau and Kelly, 2010) humanitarianism, which refocused without changing the origin and character of societal power exerted upon criminals. Jeremy

Bentham's vision of the Panopticon prison is cited (Semple, 1993) as an exact representation of this power.

In the contemporary theory of punishment developed in the 1950s, analytic philosophers in the Anglo-American tradition all embraced (and continue to embrace) a few essential conceptual features, embodied by John Rawls (1955) in America and H. L. A. Hart (1959) in England. They separated the definition from the justification of punishment: the former should not guarantee the latter, and the latter should not preclude the former. They separated justifying the practice of punishment from justifying any specific act of punishment: the former can exist without the latter. Practice of punishment is justified based on social values, goals, etc.; acts of punishment are justified based on norms (principles/standards/rules). Punishment practice is justified consequentially, e.g., as preventing/decreasing crime to increase social welfare, as in utilitarianism; deontologically, e.g., as retribution, as a good per se or as justice requires; or both. Foucault, however, disregards these analytical features in his discussion of theory and practice of punishment. He reflects on and reinterprets human nature, public institutions, and the purposes of punishment practices on a broad scale in favor of empirical hypotheses, normative or conceptual analyses, or principles as bases for policies.

Whereas other contemporary theorists of punishment (cf. Rawls, Hart) propose certain grounds for justifying the practice of punishment, Foucault's views intrinsically oppose any such justification. Some (Bedau and Kelly, 2010) characterize him as a form of "paradigmatic thinker," finding his perspectives on punishment "anti-foundationalist" (as were David Hume's and Adam Smith's views on moral philosophy in general). From Foucault's perspective, like all social practices, punishment is inseparably related to ideology and its beliefs and assumptions, which lack any independent rational basis. Foucault finds thinking it is even possible to justify penal institutions highly dubious and self-deluding. Among recent authors discussing punishment practices in Western society, Bedau and Kelly (2010) see Foucault as most synthesizing anti-analytic, anti-foundationalist, and historical beliefs—resultantly generating profound misgivings about how to justify punishment, moreover whether it should be justified at all. They see Friedrich Nietzsche as an implicit influence on Foucault regarding punishment philosophy, because Nietzsche viewed punishment as "overdetermined by utilities" (1887) and subject to varying interpretations of its purposes, due to human nature's entrenched motivations to "subordinate, coerce, transform" (Bedau and Kelly, 2010) others through punishment.

Although liberalism regarding punishment during the 18th-century Enlightenment has been found ambiguous (cf. Beccaria, 1764; Bedau and Kelly, 2010), similar liberal concepts have reappeared in contemporary theory of punishment, as represented in the 1950s by Rawls in America and Hart in England. Informed by these ideas, most philosophers have drawn two main conclusions. (1) Even though different individual acts of punishment can certainly be criticized for being inappropriate, invalid, undeserved, excessive, or brutal, it is still clear that a liberal, constitutional democracy justifies the overall practice of punishment itself. (2) Both deontological and consequential ethical factors must be included in consideration to justify the practice of punishment. Neither one nor the other will suffice by itself. Punishment seen purely as retribution is overly rigid; punishment seen as purely consequential is counterintuitive, particularly toward punishing innocent individuals. Hence the practice of punishment depends not on an exclusive value but multiple values.

One requirement of analytic philosophy for defining punishment is that the definition be value-neutral, i.e., it does not anticipate any policy issue. One potential definition (Bedau and Kelly, 2010) is that legal, non-paradigmatic punishment (e.g., of students in school, children at home, etc.) involves *depriving* individuals, by sanction, of rights such as privacy, freedom, etc.; or *imposing* burdens, for being found guilty of harming innocent persons or some other criminal violation. As Hobbes defined it, punishment emphasized imposing pain on people rather than depriving them of rights. The aforementioned summary definition of punishment as depriving people of rights or imposing burdens on them establishes some fundamental points: punishment is not accidental or incidental damage; it is authorized by the pertinent jurisdiction's political authority. Punishment involves depriving or withholding some advantage or imposing some disadvantage. More specifically, depriving an offender of *rights* mirrors the victim's rights that the offender violated, so the punishment is in kind with the harm done. Thus the loss or burden of punishment is judged overtly and objectively, not covertly or subjectively.

To meet the criterion of not prejudging any policy considerations, punishment can be defined as: (1) being legally authorized, and (2) depriving rights and/or imposing burdens. Additionally, punishment can be defined as: (3) not being a naturally occurring, external event, but a humanly established institution. People must be assigned different, socially defined roles, governed by human-made public rules, for punishment to be practiced. While variable kinds of harm can come to miscreants, these are not directly considered punishment unless personal agency administers them. Punishment is (4) given to people who are found to have behaved wrongly (though this can be disputed). People authorized to do so must find an individual guilty, and believe in the individual's guilt, to justify punishing that person. A person must not actually *be* guilty as a condition; hence punishing undeserving and innocent people is not necessarily found unjust. (5) By definition, the practice of punishment does not incorporate any one stated intention/purpose. As Nietzsche first observed, it affords multiple functions/purposes.

In addition to being (1) legally authorized; (2) depriving offenders of rights or imposing burdens on them; (3) humanly constructed, not naturally occurring; (4) administered to those found guilty by those authorized to do so and believing them guilty, but not necessarily to those actually being guilty; and (5) administered not for any single purpose, but several; a value-neutral (not anticipating, guaranteeing, or prejudging any question of policy) definition of punishment also (6) does not include all socially sanctioned deprivations, but only those made to punish findings of criminal guilt (as opposed to contract breaches, torts, or subject to taxation or licensing charges). Punitive deprivations are distinguished from non-punitive ones in that non-punitive deprivations do not demonstrate "social condemnation" (Feinberg, 1965; Bedau, 2001). This condemnation is not extrinsic, but intrinsic to the practice of punishment. (7) Punishment by "authorized deprivation" includes parental/adult punishments of children, albeit more ambiguous than legal punishment because most humans learn about such punishment far prior to any legal confrontations.

Punishment, particularly governmentally authorized legal punishment, is not a natural event but an institution that human beings have constructed, intentionally and deliberately organized, and now consciously practices. However, this does not also mean that punishment is a social institution that all societies universally require. It is not evidence of conditions that are needed for human beings to cooperate socially, but rather evidence of human fallibility. In spite of the beliefs of many authors, ranging from Bishop Joseph Butler

(1723) to Sir Peter Strawson (1962) that humanly instituted and practiced punishment is more closely related to the natural resentment typically evoked by unwarranted aggressive actions, or to acts of retaliation or other aggression observed in non-human animals, this potential justification of punishment denies those beliefs in favor of its finding the only relationship of humanly designed and implemented punishment to those reactions to be biological and/or historical in nature, and nothing more.

In terms of empirical evidence or conceptual principles, one position maintains that punishment as either an institution or a practice, or as both, is not actually necessary to human societies. Although this position concedes that it may be impracticable for human societies to operate without incorporating the practice of punishment in some way, it still insists that the existence of a human society that does not include the practice of punishment is conceivable. Furthermore, this argument allows that, when we consider the suffering that results from practicing punishment, it is even possible that, from a rational point of view, human society could even make the decision to live without the institution or practice of punishment. Consistent with the expression of this possibility, over time, some social theorists have periodically advocated for abolishing the institution and practice of punishment completely (for example, B. F. Skinner, 1948; Bedau, 1991; and A. Davis, 2003).

Punishments carried out according to governmentally enacted laws enforced by legal authorities—particularly punishments administered according to the laws in liberal constitutional democracies like the United States, regardless of what the resulting social and legal benefits are, still cause significant costs to everybody who participates in carrying out such punishments. Therefore, in any human society that purposely elects to go on administering these punishments and hence incurring those attendant costs, it becomes incumbent on its governing officials and other members to furnish some kind of rationale to justify a ratio wherein the costs outweigh the benefits. However much the society eschews exploring and experimenting with alternative social interventions regarding personal liberty, which could prove superior for redressing harm and promoting healing for crime victims and for preventing crime before it occurs, and chooses instead to continue incurring the costs of punishment, the demand for a rationale to justify this continues to be exacerbated (cf. Currie, 1985).

By its innate character, punishment entails coercive, dominating power of the people who administer acts of punishment over people who undergo those punitive actions. Philosophers remind us of the significance of this power differential. It is normal among humans to respond to punishment with either aversion, or stoic endurance, like other undesirable events. The response of Raskolnikov, the protagonist of Dostoevsky's *Crime and Punishment*, to punishment as a welcome penance; or a pathologically masochistic desire for and enjoyment of punishment, are viewed respectively as an exception to what is normal or a perversion of what is normal. A prerequisite to punishing another person is having established control over the person to be punished. Without this control, the would-be punisher will fail to punish the other. However, the power to inflict punishment is distinguished from simply harming others adventitiously: instead, it has to be politically institutionalized and authorized by the prevailing government.

Administering punishment typically has the intention of depriving the person who is punished of something, and/or of imposing some burden on that person; it typically accomplishes such deprivation and/or imposition. Because of this inherent quality of deprivation and/or burden on the person being punished, the power to punish affords the persons giving the punishment paramount opportunities for abusing their power. Therefore it is necessary to differentiate valid deprivations and/or burdens which are necessary to the nature of punishment from excessively harsh, cruel, and inhumane punishments which are not necessary. To make this distinction, those with the power to determine and administer punishment must refer to how the valid punishments are connected with, and the excessive punishments are disconnected from, the substance of the sentence involved and its justification (Bedau, 1972). This distinction applies particularly to punishments via the legal system because they are severe by nature, and their abuses are equally so.

To justify punishment, one begins by acknowledging people do not do it for its own sake like philosophy, poetry, music, or other activities wherefrom they derive inherent value, but for some purpose(s). Philosophers like Nietzsche and Foucault disagree, believing human nature involves innate, unconscious and/or camouflaged satisfaction in causing others legally authorized harm through punishment. (Foucault was informed by Freud's psychoanalytic theory, among others; Freud would agree, supplying the death drive *Thanatos* as motivation.) Other philosophers, finding such satisfaction perverse, insist practicing punishment furthers our outcomes/goals. While purpose is unnecessary to define punishment, it is necessary to justify it. Justifying punishment entails (1) identifying one's goals in practicing punishment; (2) proving these goals are accomplished through punishment; (3) proving that punishment, and certain ways of punishing, are necessary to accomplish these goals and cannot be replaced by non-punitive interventions with equal or better effectiveness; and (4) proving that accomplishing these goals via punishment is justified. All these, particularly the last step, are contestable: as justification lacks theoretical limits, designing an ideal system and/or criticizing existing punishment systems also lack theoretical foundations. Justification is inherently anti-foundationalist via its unavoidably argumentative nature.

War

War is an armed conflict between/among political communities that is real, intentional, and widespread. Hence fistfights between individuals, gang wars, or feuds between families are not wars. World Wars I and II were international and thus classical wars. America's Civil War and the many civil wars within other countries count as wars without being international. In addition to countries and states, political communities can also be terrorist organizations and similar political pressure groups because they are organized groups of people with political purposes. Many such groups also seek to become states, or to influence the development of states in some countries. A popular distinction between nations and states from Max Weber defines a nation as a group considering itself a "people" through commonly shared culture, language, ethnicity, history, and habitat(s); values and ideals; and lifestyle elements like fashion/dress, cuisine, etc. On the other hand, states are more specifically the governments regulating life in certain locales. America, England, Canada, France, etc. are both nations and states. (Many people use these terms interchangeably, but conceptually they are separate.) Contemporary nation-states are nations forming their own states.

A recent trend of nations forming their own state began in Europe, e.g., the formation of Italian and German states by the nations of Italy and Germany, etc., and then spread worldwide. Many countries whose societies feature substantial immigration are multi-national, for example America, Canada, and Australia. Civil wars among various groups within multinational countries break out at times; for example, countries in central Africa have recently been prone to civil wars when different peoples either clash over control of one state or seek separation from it, or from remote imperialist governments which disregard local ethnic and group differences. Statehood is intimately related to war, in that all war ultimately is specifically concerned with the governance of some area. When people cannot or will not agree to peaceful procedures and/or laws to decide matters such as geographical borders, who has power, which ideals predominate, which members are included and excluded, what laws are passed, who receives resources and wealth, what is taxed and amounts of taxation, what is taught in schools, etc., these issues and more are ultimately decided violently through warfare.

Carl von Clausewitz (1873) has been called the only "philosopher of war." He defined war as "an act of violence intended to compel our opponent to fulfil our will." He further compared war to a duel on "an extensive scale." In addition, von Clausewitz characterized war as "the continuation of policy by other means." This description reinforces the concept that governance is the key issue over which wars are fought. The policy that regulates life in a given land or territory is settled either through peaceful means, or otherwise by violent ones, i.e., war. In later writing, Michael Gelven (1994) defined war as inherently violent, political or communal, and vast. Brian Orend (2005) observes that war is not only the continuation of policy by other means as von Clausewitz stated, but moreover it is about governance, which creates policy, in that war resolves disagreements over governance through the deliberate application of mass force. He finds war "profoundly anthropological" in the sense that, through war, a group of people decides what happens in a given area of the world.

War's centrality to social change and human history, yet its inherent ugliness and brutality, might appear contradictory. However, this seeming paradox actually betrays an essential characteristic of human nature: the drive to dominate other people. While some find this disturbing, it might be more realistic simply to acknowledge the aggressive impulse as an inherent aspect of humanity, equally salient as impulses for peace, love, connection, sharing, helping, and other positive/pro-social interactions. Indeed, Freud identified the primary human drives as procreating and killing. War occurs throughout human experience. Contemporary responses to terrorism include the "War on Terror"—solutions to warlike actions, even metaphorically, are characterized in terms of more war. War's violence and social outcomes pose moral issues: whether war is always necessarily wrong or justified, even intelligent in some situations; whether humankind can eliminate it or it will always exist; whether it is an alterable social practice or a result of unalterable human nature; whether war can be waged sensibly and fairly or is doomed to slaughter and brutality; who should be in charge of postwar reconstruction and how to conduct it; when our society engages in war; and what our rights and responsibilities are.

Theories concerning the ethics of war can be categorized into three main traditions: realism, pacifism, and just war theory. Via just war theory, international law is another related subject area. Just war theory is grounded in a controversial core proposition that states are sometimes morally justified in using armed force. While not always morally right, war is sometimes considered so by just war theory. This concept is not simply that war is prudent politically, or shrewd, or a bold political move; it asserts the actual justice of warfare, maintaining in some circumstances the application of mass political violence is ethically appropriate. Proponents of this theory commonly cite the Allied side of World War II as an example illustrating a good and just war. Conversely, realism is deeply skeptical about applying justice or other moral concepts to foreign policy issues. Realists say states at war are motivated by national security, power, and economy, so appealing to morality is "wishful thinking" (Orend, 2005). Pacifism considers justice a valid consideration regarding war, but finds normatively that war is always contraindicated. Just war theory sometimes permits war, while pacifism always prohibits it.

St. Augustine, St. Thomas Aquinas, Hugo Grotius, Francisco Suarez, Emer de Vattel, and Francisco de Vitoria are included among the well-known philosophers associated with the tradition of just war theory. Michael Walzer is often considered the preeminent contemporary just war theorist. The most authoritative contemporary historian of the just war tradition is James T. Johnson. Just war theory's origins, as identified by Johnson, stem from a synthesis of classical Greek, Roman, and Christian ideas. Three prominent philosophers often considered the founders of just war theory are the ancient Greek Aristotle, the ancient Roman Cicero, and the 4th-century St. Augustine. The just war tradition developed a set of rules, many of which later became codified in the contemporary world as international laws to regulate armed conflicts, for example, in the United Nations Charter, the Hague Conventions, and the Geneva Conventions. Hence just war theory has had a dual and major influence on both legal and moral discourse concerning the subject of war, determining its tone and criteria.

Just war theory is typically divided into three portions. The just war theory literature refers to these in Latin as (1) *jus ad bellum*, i.e., justice toward war, which deals with the subject of going to war initially and the justice of this; (2) *jus in bello*, i.e., justice in war, which addresses the subject of the justice of human conduct during war after it has started; and (3) *jus post bellum,* i.e., justice after war, which covers the subjects of the justice of war's termination stage and the justice of peace agreements following wars. In *jus ad bellum,* the rules are most importantly addressed to the political heads of state. These leaders make the decisions to go to war and to mobilize and command their armed forces, making them accountable to the principles of *jus ad bellum.* Leaders who fail in this capacity are guilty of war crimes. The prosecutors in the Nuremberg war trials used the term "crimes against peace" to characterize initiating unjust wars. The *jus ad bellum* rules define just vs. unjust war.

Just war theory establishes six criteria that a state/political community must meet to justify resorting to war: (1) just cause, (2) right intention, (3) proper authority and public declaration, (4) last resort, (5) probability of success, and (6) proportionality. The first, just cause, is the most important, establishing the precedent for all the others. States may only initiate wars for the right reasons. The most commonly cited just causes include these: self-defense against attacks from outside; defense of others against such external attacks; protection of the innocent against aggressive, brutal regimes; and punishment for grievous wrongdoings that have not otherwise received correction or retribution. Francisco de Vitoria proposed that all such just causes as these could be included within the description of "a wrong received." Michael Walzer characterizes resistance against aggression as the single just cause for going to war; the majority of contemporary just war theorists agree with him. Using armed forces in violation of the basic rights of others is a definition of aggression.

In considering just cause for war, an important issue is whether it is necessary to wait until aggression has occurred to justify going to war in response, or whether pre-emptive strikes against anticipated aggression are justified in some cases. The just war tradition is strongly divided about this question. Francisco de Vitoria found it unacceptable to "punish someone for an offense they have yet to commit." But Michael Walzer and others proposed criteria for defining exceptions, emphasizing a state's duty to protect its people, the question of fairness, the quality and type of evidence needed, and the severity of expected aggression. A government aware of a heinous impending attack has a duty to its people to switch from defensive to offensive action—as the popular saying goes, "The best defense is a good offense." However, the issue becomes whether the pre-emptive attacker then becomes the aggressor. International law prohibits preemptive strikes without clear advance authorization from the UN Security Council. The US National Security Strategy asserts America's right to its 2003 preemptive strike on Iraq within the "War on Terror," a topic of much controversy for other nations.

The criterion of right intention specifies a state that engages in war must intend to do so only for its just cause. The right reason for war is insufficient; states must additionally have morally acceptable motivation. Ethnic hatred, revenge, or other irrational motives are unacceptable. Appropriating land or power and other ulterior motives are equally unacceptable. The only permissible right intention for resorting to war is securing and consolidating its just cause. If any other intention becomes involved, this enables moral corruption. The rule of right intention is not addressed by international law. Scholars (Orend, 2005) observe this omission is likely due to the difficulties of producing evidence to determine state intention for initiating war. The criterion of proper authority and public declaration stipulates that states wage war only once the proper authorities (typically identified in national constitutions) have followed the applicable process, made the decision, and publicly informed its citizens and enemy state(s). States not meeting this and other requirements for minimal justice cannot go to war, as they are not legitimate.

In just war theory's *jus ad bellum* rules, the criterion of last resort requires that a state can only resort to war after having exhausted diplomatic negotiation and all other plausible peaceful alternatives for resolving the dispute at hand. The seriousness of war dictates that a state must first ensure that there is no other reasonable and practical means of resisting aggression effectively before having to declare war. The criterion of probability of success dictates that a state must not resort to war if it is able to predict that going to war will not have any measurable effect on the circumstances at issue. The purpose of this criterion is to prevent violence on a mass level that will ultimately accomplish nothing. This requirement of the probability of success is not included in international law because it is considered to be biased against smaller and weaker states.

The criterion of proportionality requires that, before starting a war, a state must first conduct a kind of cost-benefit analysis in terms of universal goods vs. universal evils. The state must consider such benefits as securing the just cause, and such costs as casualties, that it expects to result from fighting a war. The benefits must be in proportion to the costs; in other words, the advantages must be "worth" the disadvantages. Because states planning or engaging in wars frequently only consider the benefits and costs to themselves, it is important to emphasize the universal costs and benefits, which includes those affecting the enemy state(s) and any innocent third parties who suffer collateral damages. Just war theory requires all six of its criteria to be met in order to justify declaring war. Considering the high stakes of any war, it is appropriate that just war theory demands this all-or-nothing satisfaction of its criteria in order to justify a declaration of war.

In the *jus ad bellum* (justice toward war) rules of just war theory, the first three criteria are (1) just cause, (2) right intention, and (3) proper authority and public declaration. Ethically,

- 70 -

these are considered deontological requirements, i.e., first-principle or duty-based rules. The duty not to commit aggression, or some other core duty, must have been violated for a war to be found just. When a war is declared in order to punish this violation of duty, that war must further respect additional duties. These are expressed in the third criterion: the war has the duty of being initiated for an ethically proper motivation, and the duty for only the proper authority to declare the war publicly before taking action. The last three criteria are (4) last resort, (5) probability of success, and (6) proportionality. Ethically, these are considered consequentialist requirements, i.e., provided the first-principle criteria have been satisfied, the state must then additionally consider the anticipated consequences of starting a war. Just war theory therefore addresses the subject of war by combining deontological and consequential ethics.

Under the just cause rule, the fundamental rights of states and of individual citizens are the two types of rights involved. According to international law, states have rights to territorial integrity, to political sovereignty, and many others. Therefore, violating these state rights by using missiles, armies, navies, marines, air forces, or other armed forces constitutes aggression. Some familiar examples of such state rights violations using armed forces include the 1939 invasion of Poland by Nazi Germany, and the 1990 invasion of Kuwait by Iraq; in both cases, the aggressors invaded their victims' territories using armed forces and usurped their governments by establishing new regimes. A critical element of aggression is that, by committing it, the aggressor relinquishes its own state rights. By forfeiting its state rights, the aggressor allows violent resistance by the victim. The aggressor does not have any right to be spared defensive warfare; moreover, its duty is to stop the aggression which violates state rights.

When a state does not commit aggression against another state outside of its own borders, but rather uses armed force against its own citizens in large-scale massacres, intervention by other states to defend the victims becomes justified. For example, in the 1970s such internal aggression occurred in Uganda and Cambodia, in 1994 in Rwanda, in 1998-1999 in Kosovo/Serbia, and in Darfur/the Sudan beginning in 2003 and continuing in a humanitarian emergency status since. According to just war theory, other armed forces' (e.g., the US') attacking for purposes of defensive intervention is justified. Aggression using armed force violates others' basic rights whether it occurs externally/across borders or internally/within borders. The aggressor forfeits its rights by initiating aggression and violating others' rights. The aggressor has no right against defensive resistance, and has a duty to cease aggression and submit to punishment. If not, defensive force by both the victims and others is justified. For effective humanitarian interventions, armed assistance from the international community is typically required, owing to the great vulnerability and disadvantage of domestic populations from their own state's violent assault.

States' rights

It appears that states have established rights in order to obtain the things to which they have human rights, and to protect their citizens. Both the Enlightenment philosopher John Locke and the Founding Fathers of the United States of America stated that people establish governments to realize the people's fundamental rights. Governments which accomplish this are valid; those which fail to do so have no reason or right to existence. From a moral perspective, only governments that are legitimate have the right to wage war, and have any rights at all. Just war theory requires such a theory of legitimate government. St. Thomas Aquinas is recognized as the preeminent member of the classical just war tradition to realize this necessity. War is, in its essence, a violent conflict over the way that people in a territory will be governed. Therefore, its association with the legitimacy of governance is consistent with this view of war.

To the question of why ethicists discussing just war theory relative to international law include state rights in their discussion, they answer with three reasons. (1) To render state rights morally legitimate rather than relegating them to discussion for their own sake. (2) To identify the moral faults of aggression and explain why responding with warfare is justified: aggression uses physical force to violate people's and communities' most basic rights—to survival, physical security, sufficient subsistence resources, living in peace, and choosing their lives and societies for themselves. Hence aggression assaults human civilization's backbone. As such, measures as serious as war are justified—assuming all other criteria of *jus ad bellum* are satisfied—for resisting aggression. (3) In civil war contexts not involving classic international aggression, explaining justice requires addressing legitimacy. When parts of a previously unified state divide against each other, morality must be determined via legitimacy, i.e., which side (if either) demonstrates minimal justice; and aims to establish/defend a valid political structure meeting the criteria for legitimate government. Membership in/support of that side is ethical.

Legitimate government according to principles of international law

According to international law principles, a legitimate government would be defined by three fundamental criteria. When these criteria are all satisfied by a state's government, that state has the right to be left in peace and the right to govern. These criteria are: (1) the international community and the state's own citizens recognize its legitimacy. General order and peace exist in its society without coercion. The state is not treated by the rest of the world as an outcast or shunned. (2) The state does not violate the rights of other valid states, and especially does not engage in aggression against them. (3) A legitimate state makes every reasonable attempt to grant its own citizens their human rights, such as their rights to life, liberty, and provisions for survival. Any state that does not meet these criteria has no right to govern or to engage in war. Theorists describe states that do satisfy these criteria as being political communities that are "minimally just" and legitimate.

Aggression as committed by terrorist groups

The concept of aggression does not inherently exclude terrorism. Just as states/nations do, terrorists also violate others' basic rights by deploying armed force. They are subject to the same rule of forfeiting their rights to avoid the consequences of defensive responses also using armed force. Terrorist acts nearly always involve aggression, because terrorism by definition uses murder and other random violence against civilians to spread fear through a population in the hope of furthering their political objectives. A prominent example is the attacks by the terrorist group Al-Qaeda against the United States on September 11, 2001. The terrorists' taking control of US airplanes, as well as subsequently using them as missiles targeting the Pentagon and World Trade Center buildings, both constituted use of armed force, violating both US state rights to territorial integrity and political sovereignty and citizen human rights to life and liberty. Al-Qaeda terrorists purposely modeled their assaults after Japan's strike on Pearl Harbor in 1941 precipitating US World War II entry. Their outright aggression justified the US response attacking Afghanistan's Taliban regime, which sponsored, financed, manned, armed, and protected Al-Qaeda, enabling its attacks.

Biotic and panbiotic ethics

Life-centered ethics is also known as biotic ethics. This division of ethics values life itself as well as the biospheres and species that exist in life. Based on these values, life-centered ethics identifies safeguarding and reproducing life as a human goal. As such, it shares principles in common with bioethics and environmental ethics, e.g., the importance of conserving the current species living in our environment. But life-centered or biotic ethics places more emphasis than environmental ethics or bioethics on the actual forms and processes that all life or biota commonly share and more value in the proteins, genes, and overall organic substance of life. All biota, including humans, have organic systems and developments to perpetuate their species; life-centered ethics thus views this reproduction as a shared, effectual purpose. By logical extension, then, the implication of the human membership in life is that protecting and furthering life is a purpose of humanity. Fundamental moral values are hence defined by this purpose, i.e., good actions preserve life and evil actions destroy life.

Biotic or life-centered ethics views life with a scientific definition of the process whereby complex organic molecular arrangements perpetuate themselves. It furthermore views the molecular processes of organic life forms as occupying a special place within the complex systems that exist in nature; within the natural laws that permit life to occur; within all of life, which is unified through its biological commonalities; and within life's unique characteristic of perpetuating itself, as organisms beget new organisms in the repeating cycle of life. The scientifically derived insights of life-centered ethics make it an approach which is congruent with religious beliefs that affirm the value of life, and which can also serve as a foundation for secular, rationally based ethics. Biotic ethics has also been extended from life on Earth to outer space in the form of panbiotic ethics, which concerns conserving and furthering life in our galaxy as well as our planet. Both biotic and panbiotic ethics, in considering ethical issues presented by how biotechnology is projected to be applied in space, have relationships to applied philosophy and applied ethics.

Some fundamental ethical issues that biotic and panbiotic ethics are concerned with include questions such as to what extent humans can alter humanity and life while still preserving them; whether it is ethically permissible for us to alter DNA and other biological substances that are the building blocks essential to life; whether it is ethically permissible for us to produce cybernetic organisms (cyborgs) or other human-machine/animal-machine hybrids; whether such creations would jeopardize organic life forms by taking their places; and the question of creating life in space and, if we could achieve this, the extent to which we should. As a general principle, biotic and panbiotic ethics might support such enterprises if their effects were to perpetuate life. The ethical counsel of these philosophies could prove crucial in the event that technological advances enable human self-design. In this event, perpetuating the will to live would be prerequisite to perpetuating life.

One way in which biotic and panbiotic ethics are similar to earlier ethical traditions is that they too have been formally developed. For example, Michael N. Mautner (cf. 1997, 2000, 2009) has published scholarly books and journal articles examining topics such as the application of life-centered ethics to the future of humankind in space (2009), ensuring the future of humans through "Seeding the Universe with Life" (2000), and "seeding star-forming clouds" (1997). Another similarity with traditional schools of ethical thought is that biotic ethics is categorized under consequentialist ethics, in that it ultimately bases moral value judgments of various actions on their consequences. Principles of biotic ethics are congruent with many principles of environmental ethics, including its subdivisions of Deep Ecology and human-centered ethics or anthropocentrism. For example, these share common emphases on the protection of currently living ecosystems and species. A difference of biotic ethics from these other fields is that its scope is more generalized in placing value in the essential processes of all current and future life rather than in specific species of life.

One way ethicists defend the validity of biotic ethics is through scientific evidence that all life is unified by the common origins, complexity, and futures all life forms share. For example, deoxyribonucleic acid (DNA) is organized into sequences that form genetic codes. These codes dictate the expression of various proteins, which, being switched on or off, stimulate or inhibit a variety of chemical interactions enabling replication of DNA sequences. This is a simplified description of a complex process resulting in the reproduction of life. All life forms having cells share common elements, e.g., cell membranes, coded DNA, complex protein structures, cellular mechanisms involving adenosine diphosphate (ADP) and adenosine triphosphate (ATP) whereby energy is converted and released, and genetic cycles. In addition to this unity of life argument, another scientifically-based defense for biotic ethics is the specialized position life occupies within nature. The laws of gravity, electromagnetism, thermodynamics, and nuclear physics that enable the existence of stars, planets, and chemical and biological processes converge to enable biological life. Moreover, this argument proposes that self-perpetuation is life's effective purpose; thus, if the universe includes life, it has purpose.

Various ethical and futurist authors (e.g., M. H. Hart, 1985; E. C. Hargrove, 1986; C. P. McKay, 1990; A. Marshall, 1993; and M. J. Fogg, 1995) have discussed ethical considerations presented by the subjects of terraforming other planets and the ethics of human life in space in general. Others (cf. Tsiolkovsky, 1928; Dyson, 1960, 1978, 1997, 1998, etc.) have predicted that, in order for human beings to adapt to life in space, they would want to effect basic changes in their own biological makeup. For example, people might need to engineer ways of adapting to zero gravity and low-gravity conditions; of resistance against radiation; and of producing artificial organs, robotic organs, organs capable of performing photosynthesis, and organs that function as solar sails. These discussions have prompted the ethical question to what extent we can modify life, and particularly human life, and still preserve it. This includes questions whether humankind will survive if humans are modified in such ways, and whether our intent is the preservation or evolution of our species.

While biotic ethics considers the possibility that even many significant and essential alterations to our basic biochemistry could be ethically defensible if they promoted the preservation and continuation of life, another related topic that biotic ethics never approves of is the replacement of organic human life by machines, including robots. Regardless whether robotically constructed devices that resemble living beings could prove more durable and even more intelligent in some ways than human beings, according to biotic ethics, the most quintessentially evil act is to eradicate organic life by any means and for any purpose. Hence replacing people with robots would never be ethically permissible by biotic ethics. Although this field of ethics concedes that robots can have their uses for humans, ultimately our biologically-based brains should retain the control over them and other machines, because as organic beings, humans have a vested interest in creating and continuing our organic life forms.

Ethicists have considered whether our potentially using technology to enable humans to adapt to life in space would be consistent with the purpose of life perceived by biotic ethics: to preserve and perpetuate itself. In other words, asking whether using science to influence evolution constitutes the preservation and perpetuation of life. One position of biotic ethics is that even in advanced, "post-human" beings that science could possibly create, natural human genetic structures and processes would be both maintained and extended. This position finds that the results of such engineered evolution would be comparable to the results of natural evolution, and would accomplish the same purpose of preventing the extinction of the human species. According to some theorists (cf. Kool, 2003; Kirby and Kisling, 2008; Freemont and Kitney, 2012), scientists could synthesize amino acids with which to design new proteins; develop new nucleic acids; and transform DNA into XNA, modifying our essential proteins and genetic processes. This raises the question whether our organic life form would continue thus modified. If such changes promoted survival and procreation, biotic ethics might accept them.

Both biotic ethics and panbiotic ethics advocate the maximization of life through the use of outer space. Astroecology experiments have demonstrated that the compositions of meteorites and asteroids are capable of supporting human life, on the order of thousands of trillions within our solar system and trillions of trillions within the Milky Way galaxy. Based on these findings, scientists speculate that, in the future, if all matter could become either the matrix supporting life or live biomass itself, this could enable life to fulfill all of its ultimate potential. Because biotic ethics values and promotes maximizing life, by extension it supports expanding life. The idea of "directed panspermia," i.e., seeding other solar planetary systems with life, is considered a means of such life expansion. The accelerated development of higher evolutionary forms through eukaryotic spores is envisioned. A variety of encapsulated microorganisms could be sent via solar sails to star-forming clouds or neighboring stars.

When considering the possibilities of seeding star-forming clouds and stars nearest to our solar system to populate space with life, scientists have addressed the ethical concern of existing alien life forms and how to avoid compromising or interfering with them. They point out that, if such seeding attempts are focused on solar systems that are earlier in their development, life there would either not have developed yet or, if it had, would consist of only rudimentary life forms, with more advanced life forms not having had time to evolve. They have also considered the future of our Sun, which though long relative to a human life is still ultimately finite: according to the observed cycle of all stars, it will eventually explode in its nova phase. They also point out that extending biological life, including human life, to space as an alternative to this certain demise of our solar system is preferable to protecting alien life—if it exists, which we do not know yet.

According to biotic ethics, our inherent nature as living beings involves ensuring our survival and reproduction. As part of our nature, these processes are also ethically our purposes and our duties. When scientists and ethicists discuss the possibilities of intelligent life existing on other planets, and of humans' seeding other star systems and planets with life, they consider that, if life does exist, humans could avoid interfering with it through targeted seeding of younger solar systems. If other intelligent life does not exist, then it would be the humans' responsibility to ensure that life continues. This commitment is expressed by biotic ethics. Promoting life beyond Earth, as panbiotic ethics advocates, could also be facilitated if human seeding efforts result in the evolution of additional intelligent life forms. These beings could develop civilizations that would then in turn also foster life in other parts of the galaxy. Such continuing propagation of life would fulfill the purposes and commitment of panbiotic ethics.

Deep Ecology perspectives, human-centered perspectives, and environmental ethics

The green, ecological, and environmental movements are founded on the Deep Ecology philosophy, as is the environmental ethics system that emphasizes living simply, controlling the human population, and preserving the wilderness. Viewing the world more holistically than human-centered perspectives, Deep Ecology sees human beings not as most important within the natural order, but as just one of many parts of a whole. That whole is the ecosystem, and its parts function interdependently. Deep Ecology thus differs from anthropocentric environmentalism, which focuses on conserving the environment for human needs and uses. Instead of the instrumental, utilitarian view of human-centered ethics that the environment must be preserved for human benefit, deep ecology sees the environment as having its own separate, inalienable, legal rights to life and well-being, just as humans do—but independently of them. It values all life, regardless of its instrumental utility for humans. Further, human beings' destroying or interfering with the natural world threatens not just their own existence, but that of all living organisms and the natural order itself.

Biotic ethics values all biological life forms, including those that may exist in the future. Deep Ecology and biocentric ethics both emphasize the preservation of existing species of life and ecosystems. The values and goals of these perspectives are compatible in their interest for protecting and continuing life. Biotic ethics holds the continuation of life itself as paramount. Hence it approves of the survival of human life; however, it does not find specifically human survival an absolute requirement, provided life goes on in some form. An exception to this is related to extending future human survival after the Sun ceases to exist: human technology would be necessary to enable humans to live beyond this point. In this sense, human or "post-human" survival is regarded by biotic ethics as required for preserving and perpetuating life. Additionally, humans are motivated to do these by wanting to further the conscious enjoyment of life enabled through sentience. The resulting interdependence of humanity with all life is a view consistent with those of Deep Ecology and life-centered perspectives. Biotic ethics attributes a cosmic purpose to human existence through the future of life, which humans can secure.

Many environmental ethicists identify with a position emphasizing the importance of the environment over the importance of people, and thus prefer not to be perceived as anthropocentric. However, others (cf. Cochrane, 2007) have observed that various authors (e.g., Blackstone, 1972; Passmore, 1974; O'Neill, 1997; Gewirth, 2001) have articulated logical theories of environmental ethics with human-centered orientations. It can be argued that human-centered environmental ethics are only natural because so many human concerns about the environment are motivated primarily by concern for impact on humans. For instance, the loss of wilderness signifies a human loss of beauty and inspiration, the loss of biodiversity causes the human loss of potential medicinal sources, the loss of natural resources jeopardizes human standards of living, climate change jeopardizes human habitats, and environmental pollution damages human health. Therefore, human-centered environmental ethics propose that human well-being and benefit are the reasons for our duty to respect and care for the environment.

Rachel Carson first created public awareness of the perils of chemical pesticides to wildlife, environment, and public health with her book *Silent Spring* (1962). Paul Ehrlich likewise brought attention to how the human population explosion jeopardized natural resources in *The Population Bomb* (1968). As these and other concerns were addressed in the development of the environmental movement, environmental ethics developed in response as a philosophical discipline during the 1970s. The purpose of environmental ethics is to define our moral duties relative to environmentalist concerns. Two basic questions that environmental ethics is charged with addressing are: (1) what are human beings' duties regarding the environment? And (2) why are they our duties? Philosophers find that typically, we must answer the second question before the first: to identify our duties, we must think about our reasons for having them. For instance, they could be to today's humans, to future humans, or to other members of the environment, regardless of any considerations about how human beings would benefit.

Human-centeredness has a different meaning within environmental ethics than it does regarding ethics in general. In a sense, ethics overall must be defined as human-centered, because humans are the only beings (insofar as we know) who can reflect and reason about ethical issues. This makes all ethical discussion necessarily human-centered. By contrast, though, within the field of environmental ethics, human-centeredness typically makes more specific reference to an ethical framework that assigns only human beings a "moral standing." In other words, only human beings can be considered morally in and of themselves. This means that all of our direct moral duties, including duties in relation to the environment, are obligations that we owe to our fellow members of the human species. Considering any specific environmental ethic, the most basic question may be which duties we have related to the natural environment. If an ethic answers that our duty is to protect it to prevent our own demise, this defines that ethic as human-centered.

Exclusive of environmental ethics, other ethical traditions in western philosophy are commonly human-centered. Because human-centered ethics maintain that human beings are the only ones that can be considered morally in their own right, all of our moral duties are to our fellow humans. In human-centered environmental ethics, this principle is extended to our moral duties regarding the environment, which are also owed to other humans. However, many other environmental ethicists have been critical of this perspective. They argue that ethics must extend farther than the human race itself on the grounds that the natural world of non-human beings and entities are equally deserving of moral standing. Some of these theorists find such moral standing should be extended to sentient animals. Some believe moral standing must further be accorded to all living organisms. Others find that all species, rivers, ecosystems and other holistic entities should be included. Such ethics obligate us to owe respect for the environment to all members of the environment rather than other humans only. Thus, human-centered vs. non-human-centered thinking yields differing definitions of our environmental duties.

Though it might seem paradoxical for human-centered ethics to extend moral standing beyond humans, this is nonetheless true of environmental ethics that are human-centered in one specific sense: not the extension of moral standing to non-human organisms or entities, but rather the extension beyond currently existing human beings to human beings who are not yet in existence, i.e., human beings of the future. Because climate change, depletion of natural resources, and other environmental problems will have much more impact upon human beings living in the future than they have on human beings living in the present, philosophers have found it a necessity to accord moral standing to the human generations to come. In addition, they take into account the fact that whichever policies and activities human beings implement in the present will result in significant impacts on the well-being of human beings in the future. Some philosophers, informed by these considerations, therefore base their environmental ethics on present humans' duties to future generations of humans.

In defining our environmental obligations as owed to other humans, including future generations, some philosophers assert future humans have moral standing, while others claim they cannot justify them. Some, saying we can benefit future generations but they cannot benefit us in return, deny them moral standing because, unable to reciprocate, they exist outside of our moral community (cf. Golding, 1972). Yet others cite common instances of other obligations to people who cannot reciprocate, like having to execute their wills, etc.; we discharge these obligations without considering their lack of reciprocity controversial (Kavka, 1978). Still others (Gewirth, 2001) argue that, even though future generations cannot benefit previous ones, they can still benefit those that will follow, signifying larger-scale transgenerational reciprocity. Another argument is the "non-identify problem" (Parfit, 1984): we cannot be obligated to future individuals, or give them moral standing, because they do not yet exist, so we do not know who they will be. Moreover, what we do influences their future identities and circumstances. Relevantly to environmental ethics, future generations would not exist without our actions, so they could not validly blame our environmentally destructive policies and actions for harming them.

Human rights

Human rights can be defined as norms indicating conditions and activities to which all people are entitled. Their purpose is protecting all humans from abuse socially, legally, and politically. Some examples include the right to be active politically, the right to fair court trial if accused of a crime, and the right against torture. Human rights are global, national, legal, and moral. Historically, England's Magna Carta (1215) was a significant source documenting human rights. The English Bill of Rights (1689) followed, as well as France's Declaration of the Rights of Man and the Citizen (1789), partly inspired by the American Revolution, prompted by the French Revolution and an initial preparation for a French constitution. Philosophers historically known for writing about the concept of human rights included Francisco Suarez (1548-1617), Hugo Grotius (1583-1645), Samuel Pufendorf (1632-1694), John Locke (1632-1704), and Immanuel Kant (1724-1804). In contemporary times, the United Nations' Universal Declaration of Human Rights (1948) was a key document of the human rights concept; many additional treaties and documents of human rights ensued from the UN, Council of Europe, Organization of American States, African Union and other global organizations.

Questions concerning the very existence of human rights, assuming they do exist, their content, their nature, their being universal, ways of justifying them, and their legal status are all topics that are addressed by the philosophy of human rights. The strongest assertions that philosophers have frequently made in the name of human rights include that they are moral norms that are justified, that such ethical norms exist apart from any laws enacted by governments, and that human rights are universal. These claims have often been doubted and criticized by various authors, and their critiques have equally as often been met with arguments by philosophers defending them. As a result of these exchanges, an entire body of literature and an accompanying distinct field within the disciplines of political and legal philosophy have developed a devotion exclusively to this ongoing argument over the matter, existence, nature, justification, and status of human rights.

The most basic defining characteristic of human rights is that they are rights. While this may seem overly obvious, the actual import of this statement bears examination. All or the majority of human rights are "claim" rights; that is, they dictate responsibilities or obligations on those to whom they are addressed. For those entitled to them, rights involve some status, benefit, freedom, or protection. The obligations accompanying human rights frequently dictate actions which protect, provide, facilitate, and accord respect. In terms of requiring those addressed to fulfill duties, rights are typically mandatory; however, some human rights laws appear only to state goals having high priority and delegate responsibility for gradually implementing them. Although such goals may not be considered rights, some philosophers (Feinberg, 1973; Beitz, 2009; Nickel, 2013) find it more useful to acknowledge the utility, albeit weakness, of such laws. Human rights may involve international legal rights; national, legal, constitutional, or civil rights; moral norms justified by powerful rationales; or commonly shared norms regarding human morality. Some human rights advocates view human rights as all four of these.

In addition to their involving claims of responsibilities, duties, freedoms, benefits, protections, and statuses, another defining characteristic of human rights is that they are plural. One might logically defend asserting the existence of only a single human right, for example one abstract concept of a general human right as an underlying premise; and a series of multiple, more specific human rights generated from this central concept. However, it would be more difficult to defend logically the idea of only one specific human right, for example the right to peaceful assembly, because human rights are plural by nature in addressing plural problems typically arising in human life by preventing or resolving violations or abuses of humanity. For example, human rights have been involved in abolishing slavery, prohibiting genocide, and ensuring fair trials and education (though these violations and abuses still exist in the world). Some philosophers (cf. Cohen, 2004; Ignatieff, 2004) even affirm human rights plurality while defining those rights as numbering very few.

Philosophers have identified, along with claims of duties and benefits and plurality, universality as an essential defining feature of human rights. In other words, they define human rights as belonging to all living human beings, not limited to members of certain countries, religions, social classes, economic levels, or other individuals. The concept of universality incorporates the idea of independent existence. This means that, regardless whether a given country or culture accords or affirms human rights within its morality, laws, or practices, its people have human rights independently of those. Still, philosophers note three qualifications to the concept of universality: (1) some human rights, for example the right to vote, apply only to residents of a country, voting within the country of citizenship, and adults but not children. (2) While the right to freedom of movement is a human right, this can be temporarily or permanently curtailed by imprisonment for persons convicted of major crimes. (3) Some human rights treaties focusing on rights of children, women, minorities, indigenous peoples and other vulnerable groups have less universal natures.

High priority is considered a basic defining characteristic of human rights, as well as claims of freedoms, protections, other benefits, duties, and plurality and universality. For example, Maurice Cranston (1967) wrote of the "paramount importance" of human rights, and the "grave affront to justice" involved in violating them. The rationale for the high priority of human rights is that they would not be able to compete with individual self-determination, national self-determination, national security, national stability, national and world prosperity, and other similarly important issues if they were not accorded such high priority. However, this high priority does not automatically make human rights an absolute set of values or rules. Rather, they are to be viewed as somewhat relative—"resistant to trade-offs, but not too resistant" (Griffin, 2008). Also, within human rights themselves, some variations in priority among specific rights occurs. For instance, if the right to privacy and the right to life encounter a conflict, typically the right to life will take priority.

Inalienable rights are defined not as absolute rights or rights irrevocable by other priorities. Rather, inalienable means people cannot lose or give up their rights. Certain human rights have been deemed inalienable; for example, the United States Declaration of Independence famously identified "Life, Liberty and the pursuit of Happiness" as "certain unalienable Rights" with which "men" "are endowed by their Creator." However, philosophers find it dubious that *all* human rights can or should be inalienable, where this is defined as meaning that a human being cannot temporarily or permanently lose these rights, either by voluntarily relinquishing them or by losing them as punishment for illegal or unacceptable conduct. For example, upholding both human rights and laws dictating incarceration to punish significant crimes requires accepting that people convicted of such crimes can forfeit their right to freedom of movement. While some philosophers express stronger views regarding inalienability (cf. Donnelly, 2003), others (cf. Nickel, 2013) suggest that characterizing human rights simply as "very hard to lose" might suffice.

Various philosophers (e.g., Rawls, 1999; Cohen, 2004; Ignatieff, 2005; Nickel, 2007) have found human rights minimal in that they are neither overly demanding nor very many, i.e., not thousands or hundreds but a few dozen. According to some (Nickel, 2013), this implies human rights ought to be, or are, less occupied with accomplishing the best than preventing the worst. Some have described human rights as not dealing with "great aspirations and exalted ideals," but instead with the "lower limits on tolerable human conduct" (Shue, 1996). By dictating such modest standards, human rights enable the democratic process to make local and national decisions regarding policies and laws. This not only permits ample room for national democratic decision-making, but also confers plenty of institutional and cultural variation, as well as high priority, upon human rights. Nonetheless, some philosophers (cf. Brems, 2009; Raz, 2010) criticize the idea of human rights as minimal standards. Others find minimalism does not contradict the notion of an extensive number of human rights, viewing minimalism as a norm for international human rights rather than definitive of overall human rights (Nickel, 2013).

When philosophers approach human rights theory from the orientation of ethics, they may proceed from the assumption that moral right, and not legal rights, must provide the foundation for human rights. However, other philosophers (cf. Nickel, 2013) assert that believing in human rights only when they are manifested in the form of international and/or national legal rights does not contradict the existence or validity of human rights. Some even assert further that human politics have made human rights into laws: Henkin (1978) has written, "Political forces have mooted the principal philosophical objections, bridging the chasm between natural and positive law by converting natural human rights into positive legal rights." However, one caveat involved in taking the theoretical position that legal rights are the only actual human rights is that this position effectively weakens the holders' capacities to interpret independent existence, universality, and similar such qualities as being defining characteristics of human rights.

Whereas some theorists view human rights as founded in some moral reality that they propose exists independently, others may view them instead as being norms that people have established to utilize as parts of the political practices they have developed or constructed. This latter view would assign different international or national political roles to human rights, thus according them the function of protecting human and/or national interests of an urgent nature. For example, human rights could play political roles such as defining when it is permitted to deploy military interventions, impose economic sanctions, or establish global standards for evaluations of how various governments in the world treat their people. Rawls (1999), Beitz (2009), and others have strongly advocated this definition of human rights as serving political functions in addition to the four basic definitions of human rights as claiming benefits and duties, being plural, being universal, and taking high priority.

In light of the way that international human rights have ascended in legal and political importance over recent decades, the view of human rights as serving legal and political functions seems particularly applicable. However, some theorists (cf. Tasioulas, 2012; Nickel, 2013) propose human rights still exist and operate beyond contexts of international law and politics, illustrating with imaginary scenarios. For example, if Earth were struck by an asteroid wiping out human life in all but one country, this remaining state would continue accepting the concept of human rights and practicing its provisions—even though international relations, law, and politics would no longer exist. Moreover, if it were then discovered some people in a neighboring country had also survived, even though they had no state or government, the first country would still know to treat those stateless individuals according to human rights principles. Hence the definition of human rights should not depend on their international legal and political roles. However, even those making this argument concede that, in today's real world, international human rights do typically serve political functions.

International and national laws, enacted by governments and dictated by judicial rulings, define norms which constitute the most recognizable manner wherein human rights are seen to exist. In international law, treaties that countries have signed have converted certain norms of human rights into legal requirements. As examples, Article 4 of the European Convention and Article 8 of the International Covenant on Civil and Political Rights are both treaties that have established the human right not to be subject to slavery or servitude as law. In national law, countries have made various human rights a part of standard legal requirements through judicial decisions, legislative enactments, or nationwide customs. As one salient example, citizens of the United States have the human right not to be enslaved because the 13th Amendment to the United States Constitution legally prohibits making slaves or servants of them. While in both cases, the existence of human rights is proven legally, a common distinction is practiced in terminology only: people refer to rights integrated into international law as human rights, but more often refer to human rights integrated into national law as constitutional rights or civil rights.

A limitation of legal grounds for human rights is that these are subject to global and domestic political changes. To establish grounds more permanent and deeper than human laws, many philosophers have proposed human rights are inborn/inherent (cf. Morsink, 2009). One way to make normative status intrinsic is via divine endowment. The US

Declaration of Independence (1776) does this, stating "all men" (today we would say people) are given rights to life, liberty, and pursuit of happiness by "their Creator." This perspective establishes God as the divine lawmaker enacting these fundamental rights. One stipulation is that God-given human rights must be very abstract and general for applicability to human history, not just in recent years, but over many centuries. However, contemporary human rights are often more specific, with contemporary institutions as prerequisites—like rights to educations or fair trials. Even accepting certain natural rights as divine gifts, philosophers still require explanations of their process from the abstract and general to concrete and specific contemporary treaties, declarations, and laws. Also, theological grounds may secure human rights metaphysically but not practically, as many people are atheists.

Apart from legal or theological grounds, moral grounds are another basis for human rights. As normative behavioral imperatives supported by values and rationales, moralities appear to exist in all human populations. Specific values, e.g., the value of human life; and specific norms, e.g., prohibiting intentionally murdering an innocent individual, are features of moralities. If human rights are defined as norms that all or most real human moralities accept, this can be grounds for their existence. In this perspective, human rights are fundamental moral norms that all or the majority of acknowledged human moralities share. While this is an appealing approach, it is subject to significant problems. While in recent years, human rights have gained global acceptance with increasing speed, the world has yet to reach unanimous moral agreement about them. As evidence of this, international treaties and declarations are not designed simply to define a worldwide moral consensus, but rather to effect worldwide changes in the existing norms.

In addition to legal, theological, and moral grounds, ethical approaches can be used to explain how and why human rights exist by citing them as the foundations for human rights. For example, a common view of justified ethical philosophies is that it is always wrong for people to torture other people, and that humans therefore should enact provisions to protect against the practice of torture. The perspective of using ethical outlooks as grounds for human rights would thereby attribute the human right against torture to this ethical belief. This perspective would characterize the UN Universal Declaration of Human Rights as an effort to form a political morality that was justified—not simply describing an existing moral agreement, but attempting to achieve consensus with strongly reasonable practical and moral support. Committing to such support as objective is necessary in this perspective. Analogously to discovering physical laws of nature or of human mechanics and architecture, proponents say we can also discover what people are justified in requiring of one another and their governments.

Proponents of justifying and explaining the existence of human rights on moral grounds believe that, notwithstanding the present absence of universal consensus regarding human rights, human beings can still rationally reach agreement through commitment to a process of serious, open-minded moral inquiry and political consideration. Because of the universal nature of some essential moral values—e.g., the belief that murder of an innocent person is always wrong, or that torturing people is always wrong—some philosophers propose that some moral reasons therefore exist apart from being constructed by human beings. Based on this proposition, they find that, in combination with premises related to contemporary problems, resources, and institutions, such independently existing moral reasons can produce different moral norms than the currently enforced or accepted ones. Some (cf. Morsink, 2009) say the UN Universal Declaration of Human Rights assumes just this. One objection is that good moral and practical reasons for the existence of human rights seem inadequate. Others respond that this is not a theoretical but practical issue, which can be addressed through establishing and implementing legal norms. They find a combination of legal, moral, and practical grounds for human rights best.

To justify human rights as required, universal, and high-priority, Alan Gewirth has proposed human agency in *Human Rights: Essays on Justification and Application* (1982), arguing that effective agency and action are undeniable and indispensable for humans. Freedom and well-being are the abstract conditions for successful agency by a rational, prudent agent, who logically must reciprocally both demand these from others and respect them in others. Gewirth has found (1978, 1982, and 1996) the rights to freedom and well-being, separately and combined, function to produce many familiar equal and specific human rights. In constructing this argument, Gewirth had the intention of supplying a defense of human rights that was applicable to all human agents, and that could not be refuted or escaped. Beginning with a few facts that were difficult to argue with, plus a premise of consistency, he believed it was possible to determine these two universal human rights of freedom and well-being, and to develop from these a number of more distinct and specific rights. As some (cf. Beyleveld, 1991; Boylan, 1999) have described, a large body of critical literature has been generated in response to Gewirth's work.

In the debate whether human rights are more political or moral in nature (cf. Gilabert, 2001; Liao and Etinson, 2012), James Griffin (2008) supports the view of human rights as basically moral. What Griffin calls "autonomy," "normative agency," or "personhood" is the human capacity to conceive of and realize a worthwhile life. He defines the primary role of human rights as safeguarding this capacity, which he sees as the sole source of human dignity, and hence the foundation of human rights. Griffin believes that people value this ability to formulate, amend, and seek ideas of a worthwhile life "often more highly than even our happiness." His perspective also includes "practicalities" as a "second ground" for human rights. By preventing excessive complexities, expanding rights somewhat to enable margins of safety, and considering facts of human nature and society, practicalities clarify and delimit the boundaries of human rights. Hence Griffin identifies the universal role of human rights as the protection of normative agency, while taking practicalities into consideration.

Living life with dignity

In *Women and Human Development: The Capabilities Approach* (1995), Martha Nussbaum, taking influences from Aristotle and Marx, identifies human "capabilities," or possibilities, whereby human beings can live with dignity provided they can also exercise their uniquely human powers to realize these capabilities. She lists 10 capabilities: (1) Life – the ability to live life of a normal length and quality that is worth living. (2) Health – having adequate shelter, nourishment, and physical health including reproductive health. (3) Bodily Integrity – sovereignty over one's body, including safety from assault, abuse, or violence; the opportunity for sexual gratification; and the ability to move freely among locations. (4) Senses, Imagination, and Thought – the ability to think, reason, and imagine using one's senses, informed by sufficient education; to avoid unneeded pain, experience pleasure, seek the meaning of life, and express oneself through creating products and engaging in religious rites without fearing political repercussions. (5) Emotions – being able to have attachments to other beings or things, including loving others, grieving over their loss, and feeling/expressing justified anger.

Martha Nussbaum's Capabilities Approach lists 10 capacities she considers necessary for human beings to live lives of dignity. The first five are: (1) Life, (2) Health, (3) Bodily Integrity, (4) Senses, Imagination, and Thought, and (5) Emotions. The remaining five are: (6) Practical Reason – to formulate a concept of what the good is, and to reflect critically about this. (7) Affiliation – (a.) to have and demonstrate concern, compassion, and empathy for others; to do and experience justice; participate in friendship; and benefit from the provision by institutions of the development and protection of one's affiliations. (b.) To experience self-respect and respect, equal worth, and dignity from others. This minimally involves protection against discrimination based on race, ethnicity, nationality, religion, sex, sexuality, class, or caste; and mutual acknowledgement in work relationships. (8) Other Species – to live with and care about animals, plants, and the environment overall. (9) Play – to play, laugh, and enjoy recreational pursuits. (10) Control over Environment – (a.) Political: to participate effectively in free speech, association, and political life. (b.) Material: to own property, formally and materially; equal opportunity in seeking employment; and freedom from unjustified search and seizure.

Nussbaum's list of 10 fundamental capabilities prerequisite to full human functioning is one example of pluralistic moral and political theories that have become popular in public health and world biomedical ethics during the 21st century. Such pluralistic versions of normative theory have typically been derived from elements taken from a variety of theories. For example, the principle of respect for personal autonomy has been influenced by Kant, whose moral theory requires this. Yet as applied in bioethics, the conception of autonomy discards Kant's differentiation between autonomy and heteronomy and his metaphysics of action. The result is a broader definition of individual choice or self-determination having equal congruence with Kant's "heteronomous springs of action" and John Stuart Mill's conception of liberty. Consequentialist/utilitarian themes influenced by Mill, and extended by Dworkin (1972) and Feinberg (1986) are also identifiable in the contemporary bioethical concept of autonomy. For example, bioethicists find strong support for objecting to paternalistic medicine in a Mill-influenced utilitarian position that this is more harmful than helpful in the long term.

Advance directives in medical care

As long as individual patients are found mentally capable of making decisions regarding their medical care, the general consensus among medical practitioners is that, ethically, they must defer to the patients' decisions. When patients are not mentally capable of such decision-making, surrogates must be entrusted with medical decisions. When mentally capable patients anticipate losing their decision-making capacity in the future, they may establish advance directives to address this possibility. Advance directives can include designating a surrogate decision-maker; and/or living wills, which give instructions such as whether they would want their lives sustained and/or prolonged under certain conditions, e.g., if they are found to be in a persistent vegetative state; if recovery is not reasonably expected, etc. Advance directives prompt various ethical questions. One fundamental matter is what the criteria for decision-making capacity should be. Before identifying a need for third-party involvement—with or without advance directives—such criteria must be identified. When surrogates are required, considerations include who the surrogate should be, what the surrogate must consider in making decisions, and whether to honor an advance directive.

Chimera

A chimera is a being whose cells originate from different embryos. In 1998, scientists isolated five lines of stem cells from human embryos (human embryonic stem cells or HESC). This enabled scientists more easily to produce chimerae that combined human and non-human genetic material. This ability stimulated much ethical controversy, which was called "the other stem cell debate" (Shreeve, 2005). Five major arguments central to the chimera debate are: (1) The Unnaturalness Argument questions the morality of crossing the boundaries of natural species. (2) The Moral Confusion Argument contends that valuable cultural and social practices will be undermined by moral confusion caused by the existence of beings that cannot be conclusively be categorized as either non-human or human. (3) The Borderline-Personhood Argument, focusing on great apes species, finds their near-human genetic composition affords a moral status sufficiently high to prohibit inclusion in all/most chimeric research. (4) The Human Dignity Argument finds it compromises human dignity to give related capabilities to animals "trapped" in non-human bodies. (5) The Moral Status Framework argues against giving animals human moral status, which would then not likely be respected, considering research motivations and oversight.

Clinical medical research

Clinical research endeavors to determine whether new medical treatments constitute advances beyond existing interventions, whether they would save lives otherwise lost, and whether they would prevent damages otherwise caused. Until/unless computer models are developed sufficiently to replace research, clinicians initially test new possible methods in laboratories, and frequently use animals while doing so. This raises additional ethical issues, and often cannot be generalized or transferred to humans with the same results, thereby requiring human trials. These pose the potential for exploitation, the main ethical issue in clinical research. Exposing humans to risks to gather data for future patients' benefit allows the possibility of exploiting those exposed. The alternative of offering experimental treatments to interested existing patients is highly problematic both practically and scientifically, including manufacturer motivation to produce unproven new treatments, dosing decisions, and the possibility that reliable data regarding dangers and benefits might require hundreds/thousands of recipients. Clinical research design minimizes such problems through systematic exposure to smaller numbers of people, including seriously ill ones. Evaluating the ethics of clinical research allows moral theorists to discuss the basic issue of when exposing some individuals to risk for others' possible benefit is acceptable.

Cloning

In 1997, Scottish scientists (Wilmut et al.) announced that, by nuclear transfer of a body cell, they had cloned a sheep they named Dolly. Controversy surrounding this achievement amounted to panic in some people, who wondered if the cloning of humans might not be far behind; and if/when possible, whether this would be unwise or morally wrong. Many had long agreed that cloning should never be used for human reproduction. Those finding it a moral obligation, or at least morally acceptable, to continue research into human reproductive cloning were a distinct minority. Others not strongly against the idea still saw no need for promoting it. Since Dolly's death of a progressive lung disease at the age of six years, seven months, many jurisdictions and countries have passed/are passing laws banning human cloning. Human reproductive cloning is a criminal offense in some countries, e.g., Singapore and France. The UN 2005 Declaration on Human Cloning proposed universally banning human cloning. Nevertheless, in some countries, mammals are routinely cloned. Ethical discussions continue over cloning, for research and therapy; and for human reproduction, including safety, efficiency, harm to cloned individuals, human dignity, and religious viewpoints.

Decision-making capacity

In many parts of the western world, laws assume adults and some children meeting certain criteria have the capacity for consenting to medical treatments, participation in research trials, and other healthcare decisions for themselves. However, the precise definition of an individual's decisional capacity/lack thereof is central to healthcare ethics and law. It is also becoming more a subject of philosophical exploration independently of those fields. The capacities to make financial decisions, personal care decisions, and to be tried in a court of law also become issues at times. However, in the context of healthcare, decisional capacity is most significantly concerned with refusing or consenting to treatment. Although philosophers writing about decisional capacity find it intriguing intellectually for its combination of theoretical and practical considerations, they have yet to explore it thoroughly because it is fast-changing and heavily interdisciplinary due to the proliferation of new/different clinical assessments and methods for evaluating capacity, and because demands for law to address these developments are increasing. Hence the diverse, challenging nature of this field requires circumspection of philosophers to ensure relevant, current input.

Disability

Although philosophers have been exposed to people with disabilities since ancient times, philosophical consideration of disability was seldom and fragmentary until the last century or so. Historically, philosophers might cite disabilities as examples of life's evils/hardships; or use them to explore the relationship of human knowledge and human faculties. But philosophical interest in disability per se is a fairly new development. One possible reason is that philosophers had no terminology to define disabilities until scientific thought in the 19th century organized differences in human structure and function into classifications of deviance or abnormality. This categorization enabled philosophers to generalize about and discuss the disabled as a population. In the latter half of the 20th century, political philosophy experienced a revival of concern with eradicating or decreasing undeserved disadvantages. This movement regarded disability, which government benefits and/or medical treatment should address, as among the primary causes of these disadvantages. Subsequently, social philosophers came to view disability as a source of group identity, as well as of oppression and discrimination, like race or gender. Others argue that disability basically differs from these because of necessity; it decreases well-being.

Health and disease

Concepts of health and disease are critical to biomedical ethics, with extensive political and social ramifications. For example, both the education of physicians and the regulation of health insurance need to apply some standards to determine whether or not people are sick. Theories of well-being in ethics, explanations of the biomedical sciences in philosophy, and issues concerning function are also interrelated to concepts of health and disease. While physicians address diseases, their practices are not limited to these; e.g., prescribing contraception or performing abortions. Philosophically and scientifically, it is also very hard to identify connections between diseases and other medical issues. In modern medicine, one predominant view is of disease as abstract, basically recurring in varying specific forms among individuals (cf. Whitbeck, 1977; Carter, 2003). Philosophy has addressed illnesses, injuries, and other medical conditions more than health. While some view health as simply the absence of illness, others maintain it is moreover a positive presence. For example, the World Health Organization's (WHO) constitution defines health as a "state of complete physical, mental and social well-being and not merely the absence of disease or infirmity (1948). Philosophers have approached disease from objectivist and constructivist perspectives, and health from instrumentalist perspectives.

Informed consent

Informed consent is arguably the principle most frequently associated with biomedical ethics. During the 20th century, informed consent became preeminent in clinical practice, supplanting the historical "doctor knows best" ethos of trusting physicians' decisions with the ethos of patients being in charge of their own healthcare. In medical research involving human beings, reactions against abuse fueled requirements for informed consent. For example, the notoriously cruel experiments forcibly inflicted on humans by the Nazis were met by the response of the Nuremburg Code of Research Ethics, which state that "The voluntary consent of the human subject is absolutely essential." However, ethical questions include whether informed consent should be mandatory at the expense of the patient's health; the status, scope, and content of the informed consent requirement; and how informed consent in biomedical ethics is related to consent in political philosophy, business ethics, and sexual ethics. Arguments for informed consent include protection, autonomy, preventing abuse, promoting trust, supporting self-ownership, avoiding domination, and respecting personal integrity. Problems with informed consent include deception, lying, and partial disclosures; patient comprehension deficits; coercion; undue inducement; and exclusively bad alternatives. Exceptions to informed consent include certain public health policies, risky experiments, and benign interventions.

Inequity in American healthcare and global health

Research analyzing mortality in the "eight Americas" (Murray et al., 2006) found Asian-American men had life expectancies 15.4 years longer than high-risk urban African-American men, making them the best-off and worst-off male American groups, respectively; Asian-American women had life expectancies 12.8 years longer than low-income, rural southern African-American women. These inequalities appear "seriously unjust" (Sreenivasan, 2014). Global inequalities are comparable: the global life expectancy was 70 years in 2011, but in 19 countries it was 15 or more years shorter. Moreover, that global average was 13 years shorter than in Switzerland and Japan, which, according to the World Health Organization (WHO, 2013) had the highest national average life expectancies. However, some such inequities do not appear unjust: for instance, all American women had a life expectancy of 80.9 years in 2010, while all American men had one of 76.3 years. Because some health inequalities are not unjust, then logically, health inequalities in themselves are not unjust. Exploring whether health inequalities differ from other inequalities relative to justice involves: (1) an extensive empirical literature on underlying health determinants, and (2) a comparably less developed philosophical literature on the ethics of population health.

Access to healthcare and justice

Most developed nations offer universal access to a wide variety of public and private health services. Ethical questions include whether social justice requires access to healthcare, or countries offer/do not offer it according to social policy. If healthcare access is a social justice requirement, then it is incumbent upon societies to define what types of healthcare they owe citizens, and what they owe if unable to satisfy every health need. Considering the variety of obstacles to healthcare access, people must define what appropriate access to healthcare is. They must explain why these obligations are matters of justice. Various descriptions of social justice necessarily characterize such healthcare duties differently. If universal healthcare access cannot ensure health equality, ethicists (Daniels, 2013) question whether universal access is a justice requirement. Consequences of unequal access to healthcare can exacerbate the results of unequal distributions of other health determinants. Justice concerns affect judgments regarding both equitable and equal access. Ethicists ask what kinds of healthcare we owe one another. They also question whether, in light of their views of justice, we have a right to healthcare or health and, if so, which entitlements that right dictates.

Pregnancy and childbirth

Philosophers have primarily concentrated on abortion, and secondarily on different technologies for assisted reproduction, when they discuss the ethics of reproduction. But pregnancy, labor, and childbirth can entail various other difficult ethical matters that are becoming more important to biomedical ethics. Philosophy of law encounters issues like whether pregnancy should be categorized legally as a disability, or what legal status is appropriate for a fetus. Some philosophers approach pregnancy from a phenomenological perspective. Some reflect theoretically on the nature of personal identity, selfhood, embodiment, and care. Because women often need medical intervention and care during pregnancy and labor, and because America and other developed countries typically "medicalize" normal pregnancies and births, some philosophers (cf. Kukla and Wayne, 2011) discuss these from a medical perspective. However, even when focusing on pregnancy and childbirth as medical processes, metaphysical, experiential, legal, and other contexts necessarily interact with medical ones. For example, the ethics of treating a fetus as a medical patient incorporates legal implications. Categories of ethical issues include: (1) obstetrical care of competent, autonomous women; (2) decisionally incompetent women/those with questionable competence; and (3) communicating and managing reproductive risk.

Privacy in medicine

Governments, institutions, and individuals generally value, protect, and practice medical privacy by honoring community and individual expectations for self-ownership, bodily integrity, intimacy, and modesty; respecting health decisions; and limiting access to health information. (1) Regardless if from fear of shame, reserve, etiquette, or personal taste, individuals typically keep health issues private. When sharing sensitive health matters, they usually do so with culturally appropriate reserve and discretion. Due to these privacy practices, governments, researchers, employers, friends, and families may not obtain all the medical information they want at the time they want it. Social/economic status in part determines individuals' practical capacity to protect and control their health privacy. Children, mentally incompetent adults, those dependent on government programs, and incarcerated adults lack such control. (2) Insurers, hospitals, practitioners, and others with access to health information subscribe to ethical codes dictating professional responsibility for confidentiality of medical records and communications. Medical providers and researchers also try to ensure patient privacy. (3) Societies require legal privacy obligations of citizens, including healthcare insurers, providers, researchers, data processors, government, and public health officials. Hence breach of confidentiality or privacy is often a legal liability. Laws include informational, physical, associational, proprietary, and decisional privacy.

Public health

Promoting and protecting population health is the essential concern of public health, which the Institute of Medicine (1988) defined as "what we, as a society, do collectively to assure the conditions in which people can be healthy." Government intervention is frequently needed/involved to serve population health. For instance, in the US, the Environmental Protection Agency, Consumer Protection Agency, Food and Drug Administration, and Centers for Disease Control and Prevention are public health agencies, partially or wholly. All US states and most counties and municipalities include health departments fulfilling a variety of functions, from collecting and utilizing epidemiological data to monitor population disease to inspecting commercial food services. The World Health Organization (WHO) is an example of promoting and protecting global population health. One perspective regarding public health ethics views an imperative for maximizing welfare as the moral basis of public health. This perspective characterizes public health's essential moral challenge as balancing positive health outcomes with individual freedoms, e.g. requiring treatment for active/infectious tuberculosis or municipal water-fluoridating policies. Another perspective views social justice as the moral basis of public health, dictating a commitment to limiting unjust inequalities and assuring adequate health to all

Organ donation

People's right to decide what happens to their bodies before and after dying is a subject for hard ethical dilemmas prompted by organ donation. Philosophers question such matters as what people's claims are regarding their bodies, what respecting these claims would entail, how these should be reconciled with their families' claims, and/or the needs of people requiring organ transplants. Knowing the pertinent facts is required to answer such questions satisfactorily, as in other applied ethics subjects. Four empirical premises regarding organ transplantation are generally accepted: (1) For many cases of organ failure, transplantation is an effective treatment. (2) Researchers have shown (cf. Machnicki et al., 2006) organ transplants are cost-effective. (3) Organ transplantation is not experimental, but routine (cf. Tilney, 2003). For example, liver, lung, heart, kidney, pancreas, and intestinal transplants are performed frequently and successfully. (4) Organs are in short supply: many patients needing transplants do not receive them. Biomedical ethics has addressed topics of retrieving organs from dead donors, from living donors, the Hippocratic Oath's "do no harm" mandate, valid consent, the moral force of consent, and live donors incompetent to give consent.

Sale of human organs

Because demand for organ transplants exceeds supply of donations, some people propose selling organs, e.g., encouraging/permitting living, consenting adults to donate kidneys for financial compensation, as a potential solution. Proponents defend organ sale based on self-ownership, libertarianism, respect for autonomy, consistency with payment for risky labor, and saving lives. Others finding it unethical, even abhorrent, call for a ban. Opposing arguments include harm, risk; undermining altruism; inducements undermining consent; and exploitation, instrumentalization, and objectification. In countries requiring prior consent to donate organs after death, organ sale can involve paying donors in advance while still alive. In countries requiring family consent, it can involve paying relatives right after donors die. Most organ sale proponents advocate a regulated market, not a free one; valid consent; reasonable payment; and provision of adequate medical care. Some (Erin and Harris, 1994; 2003) propose a policy that organ sale should be: (1) limited to a specific geopolitical region, e.g., the European Union or a state, where only residents/citizens can sell/receive organs; (2) funded and made by a central public entity responsible for these, and for allocating organs equitably according to clinical criteria, prohibiting direct sales; and (3) priced with reasonable generosity to attract voluntary donors.

Human embryonic stem cells (HESC) research

HESC research affords great potential to relieve human suffering caused by injuries and diseases. HESCs have the characteristics of being able to differentiate into all of the different kinds of cells in the body, and of being capable of renewing themselves. HESC research has the primary purposes of identifying the mechanisms regulating the differentiation of cells, and differentiating HESCs into specific types of cells with which life-threatening and debilitating injuries and illnesses can be treated. Despite its great therapeutic potential, HESC research has been strongly opposed by those who object to destroying human embryos to harvest HESCs. They are harvested *in vitro* around five days into development, when the embryo has 200-250 cells. Most of these cells make up the blastocyst's outer layer, the trophoblast. There are 30-34 cells in the blastocyst's inner mass; this is where HESCs are harvested from, which necessitates removing the trophoblast. This ends the blastocyst's potential to develop further. Opponents of HESC research find it morally unacceptable because they believe it unjustly kills innocent (potential) human beings.

Because HESCs are harvested when embryos are around five days old, debate over the ethics of this involves questions about when a human being's life actually begins; and if it has begun at this point, whether it has the moral status to have a right to live. Although disagreements over the status and value of human embryos in such early stages of development are the primary source of controversy related to HESC research, there are other ethical issues in addition to arguments about whether destroying human embryos at five days constitutes destroying human life or not. For example, some consider destroying surplus embryos produced in fertility treatment, which would be discarded anyway, acceptable. Others argue that, though illegal, researchers could potentially store these embryos or donate them to infertile couples, invalidating the claim that they are doomed to destruction regardless. Another issue is whether researchers not harvesting but utilizing HESCs have complicity in embryo destruction or not. An additional question is if creating embryos differs morally if done for research purposes or reproductive purposes. Ethicists also ask whether cloning human embryos to harvest HESCs from them is morally acceptable.

Ethical issues related to life and death that physicians have reported

Medscape conducted a 2012 ethics survey of more than 24,000 doctors practicing in over 25 specialties, finding emotional and marked divisions among them regarding the various ethical issues they often confront. Some ethical quandaries constitute battles between life and death, some entail conflicts between doctors' fulfilling their personal commitment to the value of helping patients regardless of the costs and the mandates of laws that may contradict that value, and some involve dealing with conflicts involving self-interest and/or temptation. In the Medscape survey, physicians reported ethical issues including: treating a patient when they believe it will be ineffective, generating income by conducting unnecessary medical procedures, decisions to allocate expensive resources to younger patients instead of older ones, accepting drug representatives' lunch offers, sexual and/or romantic involvement with patients, concealing errors that cause patients no harm, telling patients they believe their specialists have inferior skills, and participation in physician-assisted suicides.

In surveying over 24,000 doctors with over 25 specialties, Medscape (2012) reported Kenneth Prager, M.D., Chair of Columbia University Medical Center, NY's Medical Ethics Committee, told them that doctors encounter more ethical issues than members of other professions. Moreover, he said doctors have been confronting more complicated ethical dilemmas more often. Dr. Prager commented that nearly every interaction between doctor and patient could require some ethical decision; and that "millions" of ethical questions arise continually, which physicians experience daily. One reason for greatly increasing ethical issues is technology. A related variable is the appropriation of resources. As technology has advanced, ethical issues have increased. As an example, the question of whether to tell a patient s/he has cancer or not has always existed, but medical access to technically more advanced diagnostic, procedural, and surgical options begs the question of when it is appropriate to use these. Increasing human longevity also poses ethical questions more often, as a central mandate has become appropriateness of resource uses and expenses.

According to a physician chairing a medical ethics committee at a major hospital, a primary medical consideration today is that, with technological progress and economic realities, hospital and clinic budgets will be broken; he predicts that in this event, the government will then establish guidelines and standards for the use of technology. When this happens, "all hell will break loose" (Kenneth Prager, M.D., in Medscape, 2012). As an example, he asks whether or not a doctor should choose to order a CT scan for a patient who is not classified in a high-risk group, but whose sibling died from lung cancer. In Medscape's 2012 Ethics Survey, more than 24,000 doctors in over 25 specialties were asked, "Would you ever give life-sustaining therapy if you believed it to be futile?" Of the respondents, 35 percent said they would continue treatment, 24 percent said they would discontinue it, and 41 percent found this decision equivocal.

Asked if they would keep a patient alive if they thought treatment was futile (Medscape, 2012), some doctors responding affirmatively offered moving explanations: one saw a patient, in a prolonged coma following cardiac resuscitation that continued for 30 minutes, whose therapy was considered futile, recover unexpectedly. Several others observed that doctors "don't always know what's futile, no matter what they think," and stated "miracles do happen." Some doctors noted that it helps families to maintain patients on life support for short durations, to allow time to enable them to get to the patient, to come to terms with

- 91 -

Copyright © Mometrix Media. You have been licensed one copy of this document for personal use only. Any other reproduction or redistribution is strictly prohibited. All rights reserved.

the situation's finality, to say goodbye to the patient, and to have sufficient time for grieving. Some said futility was not the primary concern: even if treatment would not bring a cure or remission but extended the patient's life with "acceptable quality of life," their attitude was, "why not?" Many doctors pointed out the importance of advance directives in such situations.

In a 2012 large-scale ethical survey of doctors, although some responded they would continue treatment ultimately thought "futile" if it would extend the patient's life with decent quality of life, others reported that, when family members insisted on continuing such treatment, they would initiate conversations encouraging them not to do so. Columbia University Medical Center Ethics Committee Chair Kenneth Prager, M.D. said he preferred an extremely narrow definition over the term "futile." For example, he said if a patient were on life support in the hospital with multiple organ failure, and all physicians believed the patient would die in the hospital regardless of what they did, this was "not really keeping the patient alive," but rather "what I call 'prolonging the dying process.'" Dr. Prager commented "medical futility care" was not the chief strain on healthcare budgets: "Often, it's the family... being very unrealistically blind to the suffering of the patient with all the invasive treatments... and the pain he's experiencing as he's being cared for."

Some politicians opposed to enhancing government provision of healthcare access concocted stories of "death panels" to make life-or-death decisions affecting patients, which were completely untrue. However, the fact that these false claims could evoke such emotional reactions in some people demonstrated the controversial nature of issues related to doctor choices when not every patient can receive a treatment. Some doctors surveyed by Medscape (2012) stated they would require specific case details to decide whether to treat one patient over another. Of other physicians, 39 percent said they would not give a limited-supply treatment to a younger than older patient, 27 percent said they would, and 35 percent said it would depend on individual circumstances. One doctor said if he had a younger patient and an older patient who were "equally sick" with "the same chance of survival," he would "consider allocating more resources for the management of the younger patient." Regarding allocating resources among patients when demand exceeds supply, doctors also pointed out they do this nationally with organ transplant cases.

Physicians surveyed (Medscape, 2012) differed among responses whether they would or would not provide scarce/expensive treatment to a younger patient over an older one if their illnesses and prognoses were the same. One doctor acknowledged medicine and society must confront this reality, commenting, "just because costly technology is available does not necessarily mean... we should feel obliged to use it in every situation." Another doctor pointed out s/he would rather treat an "older patient contributing to society over a young psychopathic mass murderer, for example." Another physician countered that practitioners cannot determine whether a younger patient would "be 'more valuable,'" or "guarantee the younger person will live longer." Columbia University Medical Center Ethics Committee Chair Kenneth Prager, M.D. stated, "doctors should not be in the business of deciding which life has a quality worth sustaining or not," adding younger doctors tend to think elderly patients have had enough chance to live while older physicians disagree, knowing they would not want anyone "pulling the plug" on them.

In a large 2012 survey of many thousands of physicians in various specialties, Medscape asked whether they would continue treating a patient if they believed the patient had some chances of recovering but their family wanted to terminate the treatment regardless.

Although it is more common for family members to want medical means to continue the patient's life in almost every circumstance, in some cases there are families who want treatment terminated even though the doctor feels this would be premature Thirty-two percent of physicians surveyed said they would not oppose the family's wishes in such cases, 23 percent said they would, and 45 percent responded that it depended on the case. One doctor reported he once had a healthy, young female patient who required a ventilator to breathe following a drug overdose. The patient's 18-year-old son wanted to terminate treatment; this doctor continued treatment despite this. Similarly, another physician stated, "My primary responsibility is still to my patient."

When physicians were surveyed regarding life and decisions they would make for the patients they treated, one responded that s/he did not believe in euthanasia. Therefore, this doctor stated that if s/he believed a patient had a "reasonable" probability of recovering, s/he would consult the facility's ethics committee to get an opinion, or would "ask the family to find another physician if they wish to terminate care." A physician who chaired the ethics committee at a prominent medical center commented regarding family wishes about life and death decisions for patients, "Sometimes family members realize that the patient will be disabled and require lifelong medical care, and so they want to terminate treatment; yet, the termination is mostly for the family's own convenience." Many doctors surveyed confirmed discussing reasons for continuing treatment with patients' families. However, others felt the patient's family should make such decisions, even when the doctor disagreed.

When Medscape conducted a study in 2012 of many physicians practicing in a number of different specialties, they asked (among other questions) whether or not they would fight the decisions of family members to discontinue treatment if they believed the patient had reasonable odds of recovering if the treatment were continued. Some doctors believed terminating treatment was more for family convenience than patient welfare. Some said they would refuse to terminate care if treatment could help the patient recover. Some replied they would explain to the family why continuing the treatment was in the patient's best interest, and try to persuade them to continue it. Others said they believed the family had the right to make this decision even if the physician disagreed. One doctor responded, "If the family is the authorized legal guardian and it is their decision and the patient cannot express a preference, it is not my place to go against them."

In a large survey of physicians practicing in different specialties, respondents offered a range of opinions regarding life and death decisions related to continuing or discontinuing patient treatment and the wishes of patients' families to terminate treatment. While some doctors gave priority to a prognosis that treatment could enable the patient to recover and said they would fight family decisions to end treatment prematurely, others felt this decision is the family's even if the physician disagrees. Other doctors raised the issue of the patient's quality of life. Some patients are disabled or medically challenged but can survive with treatment, yet their families believe their quality of life would be so undesirable the patients would not want to live. But patients may not necessarily agree: the will to live is very strong, even with patients "in terrible condition." As a physician ethics committee chair remarked, "Very often, the person with the disability still wants to live."

According to an ethics survey by Medscape in 2012, 75 percent of physicians asked found it ethically wrong to falsify/overstate patient symptoms/conditions when filing claims/requesting prior authorizations from health insurance companies. One physician called this "a form of stealing." Another observed, "There are so many ways to increase one's fee by altering the billing information." Another opined, "Anyone who [does] this should lose their license." Thirteen percent said it would be acceptable to get insurance to cover necessary patient services. Though they were the minority, these physicians made strong supporting arguments. One commented, "If the insurance company is harming the patient, our duty is to the patient first." Another said, "To accentuate the negative symptoms, absolutely yes if the purpose is to get the patient needed services." Another pointed out, "The rules of the hospital and insurance companies are not always set up for looking out for patients' welfare." One doctor said, "We are placed in a terrible situation. I have one patient... dying because of insurance denials claiming a needed test was experimental... other patients... have suffered terribly due to insurance cookbook protocols."

In 2012, Medscape asked over 24,000 doctors practicing various specialties if they thought physician-assisted suicides should be permitted in certain situations. Forty-seven percent responded yes, 40 percent said no, and 13 percent said it depended on the circumstances. One doctor believed "Effective palliative/hospice care is the answer." Another deemed it "physician-assisted homicide" rather than suicide. Another cited the Hippocratic oath to do no harm, saying, "We are healers, not murderers or accomplices to murder." However, one doctor commented that, when a patient is terminally ill, "'suicide' is a misnomer; the only choice is... how rather than if they will soon die." This doctor had a sister with a terminal illness and reported experiencing great difficulty witnessing her suffering physical pain and her children's emotional suffering "with no end in sight." This physician's opinion was that patients with incurable terminal illnesses who were suffering should "be allowed to control their fate" rather than being made to suffer for months "with hospice attempting to control symptoms."

Ethics of practicing defensive medicine

Many physicians with various specialties were surveyed by Medscape in 2012 about ethical decisions they faced while treating their patients. Among other questions, the investigators asked them whether they ever found it ethically appropriate to perform "unnecessary" procedures to avoid malpractice suits. Some doctors stated that a procedure that prevented a lawsuit was not unnecessary. Others expressed feelings that attorneys were interested in making a profit by suing them on behalf of patients/patients' families: one doctor commented, "The lawyer down the street wants my lunch." Another physician speaking from direct experience said, "If you've ever been sued for a missed diagnosis, you absolutely never want to be in that position again, so you'll test for everything." Again, this comment reflects the idea that, in light of possible missed diagnoses, all/most diagnostic procedures cannot be considered unnecessary. And when missing diagnoses has further implications of grounds for malpractice suits, doctors are additionally motivated for more procedures toward potential diagnoses.

In a 2010 survey by Medscape of many physicians in various specialties, 61 percent responded that they found it unacceptable ethically to perform medical procedures for purposes of defensive medicine, i.e., to protect themselves from being sued for malpractice. However, in Medscape's 2012 survey, 55 percent of doctors gave the same response, showing a small (six percent) but still noticeable decrease. This indicates more doctors than previously found it acceptable to practice defensive medicine. Regardless of legislative efforts to decrease healthcare expenses, physicians still fear the threat of being sued for missing a diagnosis. So even though more than half of them found defensive medical procedures ethically unacceptable in 2012, 23 percent found them acceptable. The other 22 percent said it depended on the circumstances. However, invasive procedures are different than simply performing tests. Columbia's Medical Center Ethics Committee Chair, Kenneth Prager, M.D., said he would not perform an invasive procedure or surgery defensively: "The more invasive it is, the less ethical support for the doctor to... protect himself."

Dr. Kenneth Prager, Chair of Columbia University Medical Center's Ethics Committee in 2012, responded to a Medscape survey about conducting procedures for defensive medicine purposes—"to protect the doctor, not... the patient," e.g., ordering/performing many tests on a patient to prevent overlooking any possible diagnosis, to avert being sued for malpractice if they did miss something—that "defensive medicine can be ethically justified." He attributed this justification to the observation that "We have a lousy malpractice system." Dr. Prager said he could understand ethically justifying performing an X-ray, blood work, or similar tests for defensive medicine purposes. However, he did not find similar ethical support for more invasive procedures or operations. And other doctors found defensive medicine "just an excuse to ratchet up the fees." Some opined, "If you're careful and thoughtful in your treatment, and you document your notes, you should not have to perform defensive tests." Dr. Prager attributed the variability of ethical survey responses to the nuances and complexity of ethical issues in medicine.

Ethical issues that doctors have reported finding most difficult in their medical practice

One obstetrician surveyed cited delivering infants in the presence of the mothers' husbands when the mothers were unsure of the babies' paternity as most ethically challenging. Another obstetrician found deciding whether or not to abort a "severely compromised fetus" most difficult ethically. One doctor found it ethically hardest to report a family to social services when the parents were no longer capable to care for their 40-year-old daughter with Down syndrome, resulting in her removal from home. One physician reported finding ethical difficulty caring in the ICU for a quadriplegic who could only communicate by blinking one eye. Another physician cited recommending nursing home placement for patients who wanted to stay in their homes. A psychiatrist reported the greatest ethical problem as whether to treat a mentally ill patient until he would legally be found sane—and hence executed. One doctor's ethical dilemma was discontinuing treatment of a young, critically ill woman after septic shock had left her brain-damaged, though she might have been kept alive. A pediatrician reported a minor patient's life-threatening illness being "easily treatable but guardians refuse to consent to treatment."

In a 2012 ethics survey, asked the most difficult ethical problems they encountered, one physician responded the hardest ongoing decision was overstating patient conditions to health insurance companies: "I don't want to commit fraud but in each case the patient has benefited greatly with the correct treatment." This report of successful results requiring exaggeration reflects an inherent problem with the health insurance industry, where economically motivated underwriting contradicts practitioner commitment to patient welfare. Another doctor found "end of life decisions in the face of medical futility" most difficult. One respondent reported "recognizing the deficiencies of another physician" most ethically challenging. One found "not initiating dialysis in a patient with end of life medical issues" hardest. One cited "patients wanting futile care for themselves," another "when the family demands it for a terminally ill or brain-dead patient." A surgeon found an end-stage liver disease patient would "surely die" without a transplant but was unlikely to survive surgery, whereas that liver could "easily" save the life of another, less critically ill patient.

Another identified "having to operate to save the life of a criminal who had harmed several people."

Practice Test

Practice Questions

1. Aristotle's concept of happiness was called:
   a. euphoria
   b. eudaimonia
   c. delirium
   d. ekstasis

2. According to Aristotle, the only thing that separates humans from animals is:
   a. monogamy
   b. inherent kindness
   c. the ability to reason
   d. anhedonia

3. Socrates' idea of moral relativism could be understood as:
   a. whatever a particular community believes about a moral issue is true for the community.
   b. there are universal moral principles that are the standard for all societies.
   c. people should judge another society's moral code using the standards of their own moral code.
   d. a council of community leaders will determine the appropriate moral code for a particular community.

4. One of Socrates' central beliefs about virtues is:
   a. a misguided person may still have a single virtue.
   b. humans should acknowledge their virtues, but not fear their vices.
   c. the virtue of courage can never lead to wrong action.
   d. if a character trait is a genuine virtue, it can never lead its possessor to act wrongly.

5. Both Judaism and Christianity share:
   a. the belief that Jesus is the Messiah.
   b. the New Testament.
   c. the Vedas.
   d. the Ten Commandments.

6. The statement that most accurately represents of one of the Stoics' beliefs is:
   a. Events unfold randomly.
   b. All living things are equal in the eyes of God
   c. We have the ability to alter our circumstances with the force of will.
   d. Humans are the most special and important parts of the universe because they share reason with the divine.

7. Thomas Aquinas' idea of law is:
    a. A law is no law at all if it is not just.
    b. It is the role of the established governing body to enforce law at its own discretion.
    c. Selective enforcement is a necessary element of a free society.
    d. It is necessary at times to deprive a citizen of liberty or property for an act that is designated as criminal.

8. Who believed that the only happiness humans could experience is the temporary happiness of this life?
    a. Hobbes
    b. The Buddhists
    c. The Hindus
    d. Aquinas

9. The Libertarian way to deal with homelessness is:
    a. provide assistance for the homeless through government programs.
    b. place the responsibility on the homeless for their own predicament.
    c. provide for the homeless through privately-funded agencies.
    d. provide for the homeless with direct, personal donations.

10. "The secret of happiness is freedom. The secret of freedom is courage," was said by:
    a. Jefferson
    b. Thucydides
    c. King
    d. Rousseau

11. Noddings' term *engrossment* refers to:
    a. A. thinking about a person for the sole purpose of gaining a greater understanding of him/her.
    b. a deep fixation on an individual.
    c. an obsessive-compulsive disorder.
    d. a systematic examination of the requirements for caring.

12. The *ethics of care* are in direct contrast to:
    a. relational ethics.
    b. the interdependence of all individuals to achieve their own interests.
    c. care-based feminism.
    d. utilitarianism.

13. Epicurus is one of the most well-known:
    a. Stoics
    b. Hedonists
    c. Ethical Culturalists
    d. naturalists

14. Which statement most accurately reflects Ayn Rand's thinking?
    a. The pursuit of one's own happiness is the highest moral purpose of one's life.
    b. Humans are perpetually dependent on others to take care of their needs.
    c. God helps those who help others.
    d. True happiness comes as a result of subjugating individual needs to those of others.

15. Which of the following did Epicurus believed occurred after death?
   a. Humans suffer the wrath of the gods for even the slightest transgression.
   b. Humans are rewarded and celebrated for leading an exemplary life.
   c. Humans cease to exist and all consciousness permanently ceases.
   d. Humans are reincarnated in whatever form the gods deem as appropriate.

16. Which of the following principles is *not* one of Feinberg's four principles that might be employed to legitimize government coercion?
   a. The Offense Principle
   b. Paternalism
   c. Legal Moralism
   d. Categorical Imperative

17. Moral Egoism would encourage a person to embrace which one of the following axioms?
   a. Always look out for number one.
   b. Do unto others as you would have them do unto you.
   c. It is better to give than to receive.
   d. The meek shall inherit the earth.

18. According to Adam Smith, when people pursue their own self-interests, an unintended consequence is:
   a. societal chaos.
   b. everyone is better off.
   c. a classless society is created.
   d. financial ruin for the middle class.

19. Martin Luther King's movement of peaceful resistance was directly influenced by:
   a. Robert Kennedy.
   b. Joe Hill.
   c. Mahatma Gandhi.
   d. The Black Panthers.

20. King's most famous speech contained the statement:
   a. "Ask not what your country can do for you, but what you can do for your country."
   b. "I have a dream."
   c. "All men are created equal."
   d. "If you build it, they will come."

21. Under what circumstances would Rawls believe that economic inequality would be justified?
   a. It is essential as an incentive for greater production, increases the size of the economic pie, and enables everyone to get a bigger slice of it.
   b. Only the truly deserving are rewarded.
   c. It maintains the status quo and provides stability.
   d. People learn to achieve happiness whether or not they have economic resources.

22. According to Rawls, equality of opportunity means:
    a. Individuals always have the opportunity, under any circumstances to achieve their goals if they apply themselves.
    b. People with similar abilities and skills should have similar life opportunities.
    c. Social and economic inequalities have no bearing one's ability to advance in life.
    d. People born into a certain economic class have the same opportunity to achieve the level of success of those of the same economic class.

23. Who said, "Taxation of earnings from labor is on a par with forced labor."?
    a. Marx
    b. Jefferson
    c. Thoreau
    d. Nozick

24. Robin Hood's main philosophy could be seen as:
    a. heteronomy.
    b. economic redistribution.
    c. meta-ethics.
    d. collectivism.

25. Rousseau's idea of equality would lead him to embrace:
    a. slavery.
    b. the belief that the degrees of power and wealth should be the same for all.
    c. communism.
    d. the idea that extremes of wealth are bad for society.

26. Which statement best describes Rousseau's central tenet regarding freedom?
    a. It cannot be sustained without a certain degree of equality.
    b. It is not possible to achieve in an open society
    c. It undermines economic growth.
    d. It is not a factor in achieving equality.

27. Thucydides has been called the father of the school of political realism and scientific history for all of the following reasons, except:
    a. He was one of the first to describe international relations as anarchic and immoral.
    b. He had strict standards of evidence gathering and cause and effect analysis of events without reference to divine intervention.
    c. He wrote *The Art of War.*
    d. He viewed the relations between nations as based on might rather than right.

28. Under what circumstances did Plato approved suicide?
    a. The gods sent a sign or "compulsion".
    b. It is carried out after a sentence of the state.
    c. It is the result of an intolerable disgrace.
    d. It is committed without the gods' permission.

29. The virtue that Hobbes did *not* consider praiseworthy is:
    a. gratitude.
    b. modesty.
    c. pride.
    d. equity.

30. Jefferson's sense of "truths being self-evident" embraces the idea of:
    a. syllogism.
    b. intuitionism.
    c. Epicureanism.
    d. ethical egoism.

31. As a Stoic, Epictetus believed that all external events are determined by:
    a. the gods.
    b. people's actions.
    c. fate.
    d. other people's actions.

32. Royce's metaphysical speculation relied on:
    a. moral nihilism.
    b. formal logical and mathematical concepts.
    c. divine intervention.
    d. psychological egoism.

33. Applying Kant's Categorical Imperative, it would be morally acceptable to do all of the following, except:
    a. have an indentured servant.
    b. hire a music teacher to give piano lessons.
    c. crash your car into a wall.
    d. chop down a tree in your backyard.

34. The idea that no vengeance exacted shall exceed the original injury is known as:
    a. lex talionis.
    b. mens rea.
    c. categorical imperative.
    d. arête.

35. If someone has sex with a person who is intoxicated, the law in most states classifies that scenario as:
    a. strictly the business of the people involved.
    b. rape.
    c. the responsibility of the intoxicated person.
    d. the responsibility of the bar or restaurant who sold the person the alcohol.

36. If adultery involves deception, it is considered morally wrong according to:
    a. informed consent.
    b. divine command theory of morality.
    c. lex talionis.
    d. act utilitarianism.

37. What is one of the primary factors that has contributed to the increase in the production and consumption of pornography?
    a. Lowering the voting age
    b. The Internet
    c. Lowering the legal age for purchasing and drinking alcoholic beverages
    d. Changing the broadcast standards for network television

38. Which of the following is *not* one of the traits and characteristics that Mary Anne Warren posits are most central to the concept of personhood:
    a. The ability to reason
    b. The ability to communicate
    c. The ability to perform self-motivated activity
    d. The ability to gather food and find shelter

39. Sex selection in China and India is responsible for all of the following, except
    a. A drop in the number of boy babies
    b. A drop in the number of girl babies
    c. An increase in the number of abortions
    d. An increase in prenatal ultrasounds

40. Killing or permitting the death of a hopelessly sick or injured individual is defined as:
    a. a posteriori.
    b. ethical egoism.
    c. euthanasia.
    d. relativization.

41. Kant's view of suicide is:
    a. contrary to his Categorical Imperative.
    b. that it is acceptable if it does not cause harm to others.
    c. that if the suicide produces more total happiness than refraining from it would, then it is the right thing to do.
    d. that it is always immoral.

42. A reduction in poverty may be brought about by all of the following, except:
    a. changing child labor laws.
    b. reducing taxes.
    c. increasing general community involvement.
    d. increasing incentives for business owners.

43. The most likely result of a flat tax would be to:
    a. increase tax rates for those in the top 5% income bracket.
    b. increase the government's overall tax revenue.
    c. eliminate taxes for those making less than a specified amount.
    d. cause the nation's GDP to decline.

44. During World War II, the United States created concentration camps for:
    a. German Americans.
    b. Jews.
    c. Japanese Americans
    d. African Americans.

45. The 1896 Supreme Court decision *Plessy v. Ferguson* declared that:
    a. educational segregation was constitutional.
    b. bus seating laws violated the Fourteenth Amendment.
    c. people of African ancestry are not afforded the rights and privileges enumerated in the Constitution.
    d. race or ethnic background may be considered a "plus" in a particular applicant's file for university admission.

46. Which of the following is *not* a goal of affirmative action?
    a. Avoid preferential treatment of job applicants and those seeking school admission
    b. Increase the number of people of color who apply for jobs
    c. Change the status quo of discriminating against people of color
    d. Increase the number of people who apply for school admissions

47. Opponents of preferential treatment claim all of the following, except:
    a. preferential treatment is unfair to whites.
    b. preferential treatment leads to the selection of less-qualified applicants rather than more qualified.
    c. objective criteria are no longer used to select a candidate.
    d. preferential treatment prevents reverse discrimination.

48. The following crimes are eligible for capital punishment, except:
    a. premeditated murder.
    b. assaulting a police officer.
    c. terrorism.
    d. treason.

49. In the US criminal justice system, what is the correct order of events after the "guilty" person is identified, apprehended, charged, and held when the evidence has been assembled?
    a. He/she is sentenced, tried, convicted, punished, and indicted.
    b. He/she is tried, indicted, convicted, sentenced, and punished.
    c. He/she is indicted, tried, convicted, sentenced, and punished.
    d. He/she is punished, indicted, sentenced, tried, and convicted.

50. Which of the following is *not* one of the elements that would exclude a person from being held competent and morally responsible for his/her actions and crimes?
    a. Age
    b. Mental health
    c. Memory
    d. Intelligence

51. Who said, "Non-violence does not mean weak submission to the will of the evil-doer, but it means the putting of one's whole soul against the will of the tyrant."?
    a. Gandhi
    b. Jesus
    c. Martin Luther King, Jr.
    d. Golda Meir

52. What group believes that war is immoral, ultimately ineffective, always leads to more violence, and is never justified?
    a. Socialists
    b. Iconoclasts
    c. Anarchists
    d. Pacifists

53. From 1949 to 1989, the United States and the Soviet Union were engaged in:
    a. WWII
    b. The Cold War
    c. Glasnost
    d. A Communist take-over

54. Which was secured America's independence from England?
    a. Civil War
    b. War of 1812
    c. Battle of the Bulge
    d. Revolutionary War

55. According to Aquinas, a war is just if it is all of the following, except:
    a. declared by competent authority.
    b. fought to regain peace.
    c. fought to acquire territory.
    d. fought to dispel evil.

56. Which of the following does *not* illustrate Taylor's idea of non-basic interests of humans vs. basic interests?
    a. Bullfights
    b. Damming a river for hydroelectric power
    c. Killing reptiles and snakes for shoes
    d. Hunting for sport

57. What principle maintains that it is morally legitimate to employ coercion to protect people from themselves, whether or not they are competent adults?
    a. Ethical Egoism
    b. Paternalism
    c. Libertarian
    d. Retributionism

58. Which of the following is *not* an example of the United States using human beings as "guinea pigs" in the name of medical research?
    a. Tuskegee Syphilis Study
    b. Willowbrook Hepatitis program
    c. Nuremberg Trials
    d. Jewish Chronic Disease Hospital Cancer project

59. What government agency must approve every drug sold in America?
    a. SEC
    b. EPA
    c. FDIC
    d. FDA

60. From a utilitarian standpoint, the most important aspect of any acceptable medical research protocol is:
    a. risk/benefit ratio.
    b. funding.
    c. potential profitability.
    d. recognition from the scientific community.

Answers and Explanations

1. B: Eudaimonia is not just a momentary sense of happiness, but something far more lasting which extends throughout one's life. Aristotle did not believe that this kind of true happiness could be achieved by seeking pleasure, wealth, honor, or fame--anything that could be taken away from one's life.

2. C: Aristotle believed that humans are rational beings and should devote themselves to satisfying their curiosity, acquiring knowledge, and seeking the truth.

3. A: Socrates defined moral relativism as whatever a particular community believes about a moral issue is true for that community. That means that there are no universal moral principles that each and every society should accept. It is not possible for a community to make a mistake in its moral judgments or to have an objectively false moral belief.

4. D: If a character trait is a genuine virtue, it can never lead its possessor to act wrongly. For example, true courage would never lead a person to do anything immoral or unethical. True courage leads people to act rightfully, as they should.

5. D: The Ten Commandments, which appear in the Old Testament, are embraced by both Judaism and Christianity, while the New Testament is not. Although some Jews believe in the Messiah, they do not believe that Jesus was he. The Vedas are the sacred texts of Hinduism.

6. D: Humans are the most special and important parts of the universe because they share reason with the divine. According to the Stoics, the universe was created by God for a purpose, and everything else besides humans is designed to further their well-being.

7. A: A law is no law at all if it is not just. A central tenet of a just law is that all who are affected by it or to whom it might be applied, be made aware of it in advance of any effort to enforce it.

8. A: Hobbes was a materialist who believed that humans are composed entirely of physical matter. Consequently, temporary happiness is all that can be achieved in this life.

9. B: Place the responsibility on the homeless for their own predicament. Libertarians believe there is no way, privately or publicly, that the poor or homeless can be helped because their limitless needs will never be met. In addition, no one has the right to take away money that you earned and they did not.

10. B: Thucydides. Although Jefferson, King, and Rousseau dealt with ideas regarding freedom, they did not specifically equate freedom with happiness and courage.

11. A: Thinking about a person for the sole purpose of gaining a greater understanding of him/ her. Noddings asserts that a care-giver needs to have a sufficient idea of the personal and physical aspects of someone's situation before he/she can decide what actions involving the individual are appropriate.

12. D: Utilitarianism seeks to achieve the greatest happiness of the greatest number, regardless of the consideration of individuals.

13. B: Hedonists. Epicurus felt that if people are to thrive, they must maximize their opportunities to experience pleasure and minimize the instances of pain. Hedonism asserts that this plan is essential for achieving happiness over the course of one's life.

14. A: The pursuit of one's own happiness is the highest moral purpose of one's life. Rand did not think that humans are born to serve others under any circumstances. In her words, "He (man) must exist for his own sake, neither sacrificing himself to others nor sacrificing others to himself."

15. C: We cease to exist and all consciousness permanently ceases. Epicurus was a materialist and since he believed that the human body and soul were made up only of atoms, nothing remains after individuals die. Humans must seek happiness while they are alive.

16. D: Categorical Imperative which was Kant's assertion that humans must not act on maxims which cannot be shown to be universal laws.

17. A: Always look out for number one. Moral Egoism asserts that it's always morally acceptable for people to act on behalf of their own self-interest, which should never be sacrificed to help others or to avoid harming them.

18. B: Everyone is better off. Smith maintained that the common good is best fostered when people focus on their own private good.

19. C: Mahatma Gandhi. Both Gandhi and King believed that people should obey the just rules, but disobey the unjust ones. *Ahimsa*, non-violence, is part of the ethics of Hinduism, and Gandhi's understanding of ahimsa had love at its center. This love was extended to enemies and excluded hate and indifference. According to Gandhi, "non-violence implies love, compassion, and forgiveness."

20. B: "I have a dream." This is from Martin Luther King's speech from the steps of the Lincoln Memorial on August 28, 1983, during the March on Washington for Jobs and Freedom. It marked a turning point in the Civil Rights Movement.

21. A: It is essential as an incentive for greater production, increases the size of the economic pie, and enables everyone to get a bigger slice of it. According to Rawls, inequality benefits everyone if the ultimate result is that everyone gets a greater share with the inequality than they would gain without it.

22. B: People with similar abilities and skills should have similar life chances. Rawls believed that equal opportunity is compromised by the extent to which people are either advantaged or disadvantaged by their environment, "...their initial place in the social system, that is, irrespective of the income class into which they are born."

23. D: Nozick believed that people have a moral right to not be taxed for the purpose of reducing economic inequality, and this right should not be superseded by the goal of creating equality of outcome.

24. B: Economic redistribution occurs when wealth or income is taken from those who have a great deal of it and given to those who have very little.

25. D: Extremes of wealth are bad for society. Rousseau believed that the enormous wealth of some may lead to the abuse of those without wealth and, ultimately, the destruction of freedom. In addition, if there are extremes of poverty, the poor may become so dependent on those with more resources that they lose their freedom. Rousseau maintained that both extremes are bad for society.

26. A: It cannot be sustained without a certain degree of equality. According to Rousseau, too much inequality destroys or undermines freedom.

27. C: He wrote *The Art of War*. This text is a Chinese military treatise that was written by Sun Tzu in the 8th century B.C.

28. A: The gods sent a sign or "compulsion." Suicide was wrong if it was done without their permission or demand. However, Plato did not delineate the circumstances under which the gods would permit or require suicide.

29. C: Pride. Hobbes asserted that virtues are those characteristics which enable people to live together in peace and harmony. He believed that virtues such as gratitude, modesty, equity, and mercy "come to be praised, as the means of peaceable, sociable, and comfortable living."

30. B: Intuitionism asserts that basic moral principles are self-evident.

31. C: Fate. On the other hand, Epictetus also believed that individuals are responsible for their own actions, which they can reflect on and control through self-discipline.

32. B: Formal logical and mathematical concepts. Royce, as an absolute idealist, believed that all aspects of reality, including those we experience as disconnected or contradictory, are ultimately unified in one universal consciousness.

33. A: Have an indentured servant. Kant asserted that people are supremely valuable and should not be treated as we might treat non-human things. It is not morally acceptable to use people purely for our own purposes, as people have inherent and equal moral worth. Whenever we enter into a relationship against another person's will and their participation is not voluntary or by their own volition, we are using them in a morally unacceptable way.

34. A: Lex talionis, which means the "law of the claw." This principle presents itself in early Babylonian law, the Bible ("eye for an eye"), and early Roman law.

35. B: Rape based on the premise that the intoxicated person did not possess the capacity to consent or not consent to sex.

36. D: Act Utilitarianism is one of the few moral theories that does not contain a strong presumption against deception, breaking promises, or violating agreements.

37. B: The Internet is readily accessible and offers a high degree of anonymity. The internet has contributed to the increased production and consumption of pornography.

38. D: The ability to gather food and find shelter. The other traits or characteristics that Warren considers central to personhood are: consciousness of objects and events external and/or internal to the being, in particular the capacity to feel pain, as well as the presence of self-concepts and self-awareness.

39. A: In many parts of China and India, boy babies are strongly preferred over girl babies. Susan Sachs presents some of the reasons as "In many cultures, a boy is particularly valued as a breadwinner who will support his parents in their old age; often only a son can inherit property. A girl is seen as a burden and also requires a costly dowry when she marries." Couples who can afford it have tests to determine the sex of the fetus and may abort it if it's a girl. Some couples will even kill a newborn baby girl.

40. C: In order for an act to be considered euthanasia, mercy must be the primary motivation of the person performing it. The goal must be to prevent, reduce, or end someone's suffering, to preserve his/her dignity, or to respect his/her autonomy. If the person performing it acts or refrains from acting from primarily self-centered motives, then it is not considered euthanasia.

41. D: As Kant believes that no rational individual could consistently will suicide to be a universal law, suicide is always immoral.

42. A: This would not impact poverty and any decrease in the protection of children would also be immoral.

43. B: A flat tax, as the name implies, would create a single tax rate that would be leveled equally upon everyone regardless of income level. This would most likely mean a reduced tax rate for the top 5%. Although eliminating income tax entirely for those below a certain income level might be included as a part of the tax policy, it is not necessarily implied. Since the tax rate would be constant, regardless of income, the incentive for businesses to expand their operation and increase production of goods and services would increase, thus raising the GDP. As a result, the overall tax revenue would increase over time.

44. C: Neither German Americans nor Italian Americans were sent to concentration camps during WWII, even though the United States was at war with Germany and Italy, as well as Japan.

45. A: Educational segregation was constitutional. Thus, *Plessy v. Ferguson* allowed and propagated racial segregation in educational settings.

46. A: Affirmative action avoids preferential treatment of job applicants and those seeking school admission. One goal of affirmative action is to expressly give preferential treatment to right perceived past wrongs of underrepresented groups.

47. D: Preferential treatment prevents reverse discrimination. Affirmative action actually causes reverse discrimination.

48. B: Although this offense is considered felony assault, it is not eligible for capital punishment.

49. C: He/she is indicted, tried, convicted, sentenced, and punished.

50. C: Using memory as an excluding factor would be like using ignorance of the law as an exclusion as well.

51. A: Gandhi believed that the strength of non-violence also calls for self-restraint, perhaps the most difficult virtue. He asserted that restraining oneself from retaliating requires much more strength than giving into the impulse to retaliate.

52. D: Pacifists live their principles by refusing to participate in or have any part in war. They will not serve in the military, and they will not work in war-related industries. They believe that war violates the most fundamental moral right of innocent people, the right to life.

53. B: Even though the United States and Soviet Union were supposedly at peace, they always kept nuclear weapons pointed at each other from 1949 to 1989, and came dangerously close to firing them in the Cuban Missile Crisis of 1962.

54. D: In the 1770s, the American colonies resorted to war to secure their political independence from England.

55. C: Acquiring territory, in and of itself, has no part of a just war, as defined by Aquinas. The right intentions for a war to be fought are to regain peace and deliver the world from evil.

56. B: Taylor maintains that even if certain projects or enterprises are not critical for our continued existence or well-being, they may play such a significant a part in guaranteeing a meaningful and fulfilling life, that there is justification in sacrificing the basic interests of other living things in service of them.

57. B: According to paternalism, preventing people from harming themselves is as legitimate as preventing them from causing harm to others.

58. C: The Nuremberg Trials were war crimes trials that were held in Nuremberg, Germany after WWII. Doctors of the Third Reich were prosecuted for torturing and killing concentration camp prisoners in the course of what they called "research."

59. D: FDA-- the Food and Drug Administration.

60. A: A risk/benefit ratio involves the projected benefits, potential benefits, and possible deleterious effects of a study.

Secret Key #1 - Time is Your Greatest Enemy

Pace Yourself

Wear a watch. At the beginning of the test, check the time (or start a chronometer on your watch to count the minutes), and check the time after every few questions to make sure you are "on schedule."

If you are forced to speed up, do it efficiently. Usually one or more answer choices can be eliminated without too much difficulty. Above all, don't panic. Don't speed up and just begin guessing at random choices. By pacing yourself, and continually monitoring your progress against your watch, you will always know exactly how far ahead or behind you are with your available time. If you find that you are one minute behind on the test, don't skip one question without spending any time on it, just to catch back up. Take 15 fewer seconds on the next four questions, and after four questions you'll have caught back up. Once you catch back up, you can continue working each problem at your normal pace.

Furthermore, don't dwell on the problems that you were rushed on. If a problem was taking up too much time and you made a hurried guess, it must be difficult. The difficult questions are the ones you are most likely to miss anyway, so it isn't a big loss. It is better to end with more time than you need than to run out of time.

Lastly, sometimes it is beneficial to slow down if you are constantly getting ahead of time. You are always more likely to catch a careless mistake by working more slowly than quickly, and among very high-scoring test takers (those who are likely to have lots of time left over), careless errors affect the score more than mastery of material.

Secret Key #2 - Guessing is not Guesswork

You probably know that guessing is a good idea. Unlike other standardized tests, there is no penalty for getting a wrong answer. Even if you have no idea about a question, you still have a 20-25% chance of getting it right.

Most test takers do not understand the impact that proper guessing can have on their score. Unless you score extremely high, guessing will significantly contribute to your final score.

Monkeys Take the Test

What most test takers don't realize is that to insure that 20-25% chance, you have to guess randomly. If you put 20 monkeys in a room to take this test, assuming they answered once per question and behaved themselves, on average they would get 20-25% of the questions correct. Put 20 test takers in the room, and the average will be much lower among guessed questions. Why?

- 111 -

1. The test writers intentionally write deceptive answer choices that "look" right. A test taker has no idea about a question, so he picks the "best looking" answer, which is often wrong. The monkey has no idea what looks good and what doesn't, so it will consistently be right about 20-25% of the time.
2. Test takers will eliminate answer choices from the guessing pool based on a hunch or intuition. Simple but correct answers often get excluded, leaving a 0% chance of being correct. The monkey has no clue, and often gets lucky with the best choice.

This is why the process of elimination endorsed by most test courses is flawed and detrimental to your performance. Test takers don't guess; they make an ignorant stab in the dark that is usually worse than random.

$5 Challenge

Let me introduce one of the most valuable ideas of this course—the $5 challenge:
- *You only mark your "best guess" if you are willing to bet $5 on it.*
- *You only eliminate choices from guessing if you are willing to bet $5 on it.*

Why $5? Five dollars is an amount of money that is small yet not insignificant, and can really add up fast (20 questions could cost you $100). Likewise, each answer choice on one question of the test will have a small impact on your overall score, but it can really add up to a lot of points in the end.

The process of elimination IS valuable. The following shows your chance of guessing it right:

If you eliminate wrong answer choices until only this many remain:	Chance of getting it correct:
1	100%
2	50%
3	33%

However, if you accidentally eliminate the right answer or go on a hunch for an incorrect answer, your chances drop dramatically—to 0%. By guessing among all the answer choices, you are GUARANTEED to have a shot at the right answer.

That's why the $5 test is so valuable. If you give up the advantage and safety of a pure guess, it had better be worth the risk.

What we still haven't covered is how to be sure that whatever guess you make is truly random. Here's the easiest way:
- *Always pick the first answer choice among those remaining.*

Such a technique means that you have decided, **before you see a single test question**, exactly how you are going to guess, and since the order of choices tells you nothing about which one is correct, this guessing technique is perfectly random.

This section is not meant to scare you away from making educated guesses or eliminating choices; you just need to define when a choice is worth eliminating. The $5 test, along with a pre-defined random guessing strategy, is the best way to make sure you reap all of the benefits of guessing.

Secret Key #3 - Practice Smarter, Not Harder

Many test takers delay the test preparation process because they dread the awful amounts of practice time they think necessary to succeed on the test. We have refined an effective method that will take you only a fraction of the time.

There are a number of "obstacles" in the path to success. Among these are answering questions, finishing in time, and mastering test-taking strategies. All must be executed on the day of the test at peak performance, or your score will suffer. The test is a mental marathon that has a large impact on your future.

Just like a marathon runner, it is important to work your way up to the full challenge. So first you just worry about questions, and then time, and finally strategy:

Success Strategy

1. Find a good source for practice tests.
2. If you are willing to make a larger time investment, consider using more than one study guide. Often the different approaches of multiple authors will help you "get" difficult concepts.
3. Take a practice test with no time constraints, with all study helps, "open book." Take your time with questions and focus on applying strategies.
4. Take a practice test with time constraints, with all guides, "open book."
5. Take a final practice test without open material and with time limits.

If you have time to take more practice tests, just repeat step 5. By gradually exposing yourself to the full rigors of the test environment, you will condition your mind to the stress of test day and maximize your success.

Secret Key #4 - Prepare, Don't Procrastinate

Let me state an obvious fact: if you take the test three times, you will probably get three different scores. This is due to the way you feel on test day, the level of preparedness you have, and the version of the test you see. Despite the test writers' claims to the contrary, some versions of the test WILL be easier for you than others.

Since your future depends so much on your score, you should maximize your chances of success. In order to maximize the likelihood of success, you've got to prepare in advance. This means taking practice tests and spending time learning the information and test taking strategies you will need to succeed.

Never go take the actual test as a "practice" test, expecting that you can just take it again if you need to. Take all the practice tests you can on your own, but when you go to take the official test, be prepared, be focused, and do your best the first time!

Secret Key #5 - Test Yourself

Everyone knows that time is money. There is no need to spend too much of your time or too little of your time preparing for the test. You should only spend as much of your precious time preparing as is necessary for you to get the score you need.

Once you have taken a practice test under real conditions of time constraints, then you will know if you are ready for the test or not.

If you have scored extremely high the first time that you take the practice test, then there is not much point in spending countless hours studying. You are already there.

Benchmark your abilities by retaking practice tests and seeing how much you have improved. Once you consistently score high enough to guarantee success, then you are ready.

If you have scored well below where you need, then knuckle down and begin studying in earnest. Check your improvement regularly through the use of practice tests under real conditions. Above all, don't worry, panic, or give up. The key is perseverance!

Then, when you go to take the test, remain confident and remember how well you did on the practice tests. If you can score high enough on a practice test, then you can do the same on the real thing.

General Strategies

The most important thing you can do is to ignore your fears and jump into the test immediately. Do not be overwhelmed by any strange-sounding terms. You have to jump into the test like jumping into a pool—all at once is the easiest way.

Make Predictions

As you read and understand the question, try to guess what the answer will be. Remember that several of the answer choices are wrong, and once you begin reading them, your mind will immediately become cluttered with answer choices designed to throw you off. Your mind is typically the most focused immediately after you have read the question and digested its contents. If you can, try to predict what the correct answer will be. You may be surprised at what you can predict.

Quickly scan the choices and see if your prediction is in the listed answer choices. If it is, then you can be quite confident that you have the right answer. It still won't hurt to check the other answer choices, but most of the time, you've got it!

Answer the Question

It may seem obvious to only pick answer choices that answer the question, but the test writers can create some excellent answer choices that are wrong. Don't pick an answer just because it sounds right, or you believe it to be true. It MUST answer the question. Once you've made your selection, always go back and check it against the question and make sure that you didn't misread the question and that the answer choice does answer the question posed.

Benchmark

After you read the first answer choice, decide if you think it sounds correct or not. If it doesn't, move on to the next answer choice. If it does, mentally mark that answer choice. This doesn't mean that you've definitely selected it as your answer choice, it just means that it's the best you've seen thus far. Go ahead and read the next choice. If the next choice is worse than the one you've already selected, keep going to the next answer choice. If the next choice is better than the choice you've already selected, mentally mark the new answer choice as your best guess.

The first answer choice that you select becomes your standard. Every other answer choice must be benchmarked against that standard. That choice is correct until proven otherwise by another answer choice beating it out. Once you've decided that no other answer choice seems as good, do one final check to ensure that your answer choice answers the question posed.

Valid Information

Don't discount any of the information provided in the question. Every piece of information may be necessary to determine the correct answer. None of the information in the question is there to throw you off (while the answer choices will certainly have information to throw you off). If two seemingly unrelated topics are discussed, don't ignore either. You can be confident there is a relationship, or it wouldn't be included in the question, and you are probably going to have to determine what is that relationship to find the answer.

Avoid "Fact Traps"

Don't get distracted by a choice that is factually true. Your search is for the answer that answers the question. Stay focused and don't fall for an answer that is true but irrelevant. Always go back to the question and make sure you're choosing an answer that actually answers the question and is not just a true statement. An answer can be factually correct, but it MUST answer the question asked. Additionally, two answers can both be seemingly correct, so be sure to read all of the answer choices, and make sure that you get the one that BEST answers the question.

Milk the Question

Some of the questions may throw you completely off. They might deal with a subject you have not been exposed to, or one that you haven't reviewed in years. While your lack of

- 115 -

Copyright © Mometrix Media. You have been licensed one copy of this document for personal use only. Any other reproduction or redistribution is strictly prohibited. All rights reserved.

knowledge about the subject will be a hindrance, the question itself can give you many clues that will help you find the correct answer. Read the question carefully and look for clues. Watch particularly for adjectives and nouns describing difficult terms or words that you don't recognize. Regardless of whether you completely understand a word or not, replacing it with a synonym, either provided or one you more familiar with, may help you to understand what the questions are asking. Rather than wracking your mind about specific detailed information concerning a difficult term or word, try to use mental substitutes that are easier to understand.

The Trap of Familiarity

Don't just choose a word because you recognize it. On difficult questions, you may not recognize a number of words in the answer choices. The test writers don't put "make-believe" words on the test, so don't think that just because you only recognize all the words in one answer choice that that answer choice must be correct. If you only recognize words in one answer choice, then focus on that one. Is it correct? Try your best to determine if it is correct. If it is, that's great. If not, eliminate it. Each word and answer choice you eliminate increases your chances of getting the question correct, even if you then have to guess among the unfamiliar choices.

Eliminate Answers

Eliminate choices as soon as you realize they are wrong. But be careful! Make sure you consider all of the possible answer choices. Just because one appears right, doesn't mean that the next one won't be even better! The test writers will usually put more than one good answer choice for every question, so read all of them. Don't worry if you are stuck between two that seem right. By getting down to just two remaining possible choices, your odds are now 50/50. Rather than wasting too much time, play the odds. You are guessing, but guessing wisely because you've been able to knock out some of the answer choices that you know are wrong. If you are eliminating choices and realize that the last answer choice you are left with is also obviously wrong, don't panic. Start over and consider each choice again. There may easily be something that you missed the first time and will realize on the second pass.

Tough Questions

If you are stumped on a problem or it appears too hard or too difficult, don't waste time. Move on! Remember though, if you can quickly check for obviously incorrect answer choices, your chances of guessing correctly are greatly improved. Before you completely give up, at least try to knock out a couple of possible answers. Eliminate what you can and then guess at the remaining answer choices before moving on.

Brainstorm

If you get stuck on a difficult question, spend a few seconds quickly brainstorming. Run through the complete list of possible answer choices. Look at each choice and ask yourself, "Could this answer the question satisfactorily?" Go through each answer choice and consider it independently of the others. By systematically going through all possibilities, you may find something that you would otherwise overlook. Remember though that when you get stuck, it's important to try to keep moving.

Read Carefully

Understand the problem. Read the question and answer choices carefully. Don't miss the question because you misread the terms. You have plenty of time to read each question

- 116 -

thoroughly and make sure you understand what is being asked. Yet a happy medium must be attained, so don't waste too much time. You must read carefully, but efficiently.

Face Value

When in doubt, use common sense. Always accept the situation in the problem at face value. Don't read too much into it. These problems will not require you to make huge leaps of logic. The test writers aren't trying to throw you off with a cheap trick. If you have to go beyond creativity and make a leap of logic in order to have an answer choice answer the question, then you should look at the other answer choices. Don't overcomplicate the problem by creating theoretical relationships or explanations that will warp time or space. These are normal problems rooted in reality. It's just that the applicable relationship or explanation may not be readily apparent and you have to figure things out. Use your common sense to interpret anything that isn't clear.

Prefixes

If you're having trouble with a word in the question or answer choices, try dissecting it. Take advantage of every clue that the word might include. Prefixes and suffixes can be a huge help. Usually they allow you to determine a basic meaning. Pre- means before, post-means after, pro - is positive, de- is negative. From these prefixes and suffixes, you can get an idea of the general meaning of the word and try to put it into context. Beware though of any traps. Just because con- is the opposite of pro-, doesn't necessarily mean congress is the opposite of progress!

Hedge Phrases

Watch out for critical hedge phrases, led off with words such as "likely," "may," "can," "sometimes," "often," "almost," "mostly," "usually," "generally," "rarely," and "sometimes." Question writers insert these hedge phrases to cover every possibility. Often an answer choice will be wrong simply because it leaves no room for exception. Unless the situation calls for them, avoid answer choices that have definitive words like "exactly," and "always."

Switchback Words

Stay alert for "switchbacks." These are the words and phrases frequently used to alert you to shifts in thought. The most common switchback word is "but." Others include "although," "however," "nevertheless," "on the other hand," "even though," "while," "in spite of," "despite," and "regardless of."

New Information

Correct answer choices will rarely have completely new information included. Answer choices typically are straightforward reflections of the material asked about and will directly relate to the question. If a new piece of information is included in an answer choice that doesn't even seem to relate to the topic being asked about, then that answer choice is likely incorrect. All of the information needed to answer the question is usually provided for you in the question. You should not have to make guesses that are unsupported or choose answer choices that require unknown information that cannot be reasoned from what is given.

Time Management

On technical questions, don't get lost on the technical terms. Don't spend too much time on any one question. If you don't know what a term means, then odds are you aren't going to get much further since you don't have a dictionary. You should be able to immediately recognize whether or not you know a term. If you don't, work with the other clues that you have—the other answer choices and terms provided—but don't waste too much time trying to figure out a difficult term that you don't know.

Contextual Clues

Look for contextual clues. An answer can be right but not the correct answer. The contextual clues will help you find the answer that is most right and is correct. Understand the context in which a phrase or statement is made. This will help you make important distinctions.

Don't Panic

Panicking will not answer any questions for you; therefore, it isn't helpful. When you first see the question, if your mind goes blank, take a deep breath. Force yourself to mechanically go through the steps of solving the problem using the strategies you've learned.

Pace Yourself

Don't get clock fever. It's easy to be overwhelmed when you're looking at a page full of questions, your mind is full of random thoughts and feeling confused, and the clock is ticking down faster than you would like. Calm down and maintain the pace that you have set for yourself. As long as you are on track by monitoring your pace, you are guaranteed to have enough time for yourself. When you get to the last few minutes of the test, it may seem like you won't have enough time left, but if you only have as many questions as you should have left at that point, then you're right on track!

Answer Selection

The best way to pick an answer choice is to eliminate all of those that are wrong, until only one is left and confirm that is the correct answer. Sometimes though, an answer choice may immediately look right. Be careful! Take a second to make sure that the other choices are not equally obvious. Don't make a hasty mistake. There are only two times that you should stop before checking other answers. First is when you are positive that the answer choice you have selected is correct. Second is when time is almost out and you have to make a quick guess!

Check Your Work

Since you will probably not know every term listed and the answer to every question, it is important that you get credit for the ones that you do know. Don't miss any questions through careless mistakes. If at all possible, try to take a second to look back over your answer selection and make sure you've selected the correct answer choice and haven't made a costly careless mistake (such as marking an answer choice that you didn't mean to mark). The time it takes for this quick double check should more than pay for itself in caught mistakes.

Beware of Directly Quoted Answers

Sometimes an answer choice will repeat word for word a portion of the question or reference section. However, beware of such exact duplication. It may be a trap! More than likely, the correct choice will paraphrase or summarize a point, rather than being exactly the same wording.

- 118 -

Slang

Scientific sounding answers are better than slang ones. An answer choice that begins "To compare the outcomes..." is much more likely to be correct than one that begins "Because some people insisted..."

Extreme Statements

Avoid wild answers that throw out highly controversial ideas that are proclaimed as established fact. An answer choice that states the "process should used in certain situations, if..." is much more likely to be correct than one that states the "process should be discontinued completely." The first is a calm rational statement and doesn't even make a definitive, uncompromising stance, using a hedge word "if" to provide wiggle room, whereas the second choice is a radical idea and far more extreme.

Answer Choice Families

When you have two or more answer choices that are direct opposites or parallels, one of them is usually the correct answer. For instance, if one answer choice states "x increases" and another answer choice states "x decreases" or "y increases," then those two or three answer choices are very similar in construction and fall into the same family of answer choices. A family of answer choices consists of two or three answer choices, very similar in construction, but often with directly opposite meanings. Usually the correct answer choice will be in that family of answer choices. The "odd man out" or answer choice that doesn't seem to fit the parallel construction of the other answer choices is more likely to be incorrect.

Special Report: How to Overcome Test Anxiety

The very nature of tests caters to some level of anxiety, nervousness, or tension, just as we feel for any important event that occurs in our lives. A little bit of anxiety or nervousness can be a good thing. It helps us with motivation, and makes achievement just that much sweeter. However, too much anxiety can be a problem, especially if it hinders our ability to function and perform.

"Test anxiety," is the term that refers to the emotional reactions that some test-takers experience when faced with a test or exam. Having a fear of testing and exams is based upon a rational fear, since the test-taker's performance can shape the course of an academic career. Nevertheless, experiencing excessive fear of examinations will only interfere with the test-taker's ability to perform and chance to be successful.

There are a large variety of causes that can contribute to the development and sensation of test anxiety. These include, but are not limited to, lack of preparation and worrying about issues surrounding the test.

Lack of Preparation

Lack of preparation can be identified by the following behaviors or situations:
- Not scheduling enough time to study, and therefore cramming the night before the test or exam
- Managing time poorly, to create the sensation that there is not enough time to do everything
- Failing to organize the text information in advance, so that the study material consists of the entire text and not simply the pertinent information
- Poor overall studying habits

Worrying, on the other hand, can be related to both the test taker, or many other factors around him/her that will be affected by the results of the test. These include worrying about:
- Previous performances on similar exams, or exams in general
- How friends and other students are achieving
- The negative consequences that will result from a poor grade or failure

There are three primary elements to test anxiety. Physical components, which involve the same typical bodily reactions as those to acute anxiety (to be discussed below). Emotional factors have to do with fear or panic. Mental or cognitive issues concerning attention spans and memory abilities.

- 120 -

Copyright © Mometrix Media. You have been licensed one copy of this document for personal use only. Any other reproduction or redistribution is strictly prohibited. All rights reserved.

Physical Signals

There are many different symptoms of test anxiety, and these are not limited to mental and emotional strain. Frequently there are a range of physical signals that will let a test taker know that he/she is suffering from test anxiety. These bodily changes can include the following:

- Perspiring
- Sweaty palms
- Wet, trembling hands
- Nausea
- Dry mouth
- A knot in the stomach
- Headache
- Faintness
- Muscle tension
- Aching shoulders, back and neck
- Rapid heart beat
- Feeling too hot/cold

To recognize the sensation of test anxiety, a test-taker should monitor him/herself for the following sensations:

- The physical distress symptoms as listed above
- Emotional sensitivity, expressing emotional feelings such as the need to cry or laugh too much, or a sensation of anger or helplessness
- A decreased ability to think, causing the test-taker to blank out or have racing thoughts that are hard to organize or control.

Though most students will feel some level of anxiety when faced with a test or exam, the majority can cope with that anxiety and maintain it at a manageable level. However, those who cannot are faced with a very real and very serious condition, which can and should be controlled for the immeasurable benefit of this sufferer.

Naturally, these sensations lead to negative results for the testing experience. The most common effects of test anxiety have to do with nervousness and mental blocking.

Nervousness

Nervousness can appear in several different levels:

- The test-taker's difficulty, or even inability to read and understand the questions on the test
- The difficulty or inability to organize thoughts to a coherent form
- The difficulty or inability to recall key words and concepts relating to the testing questions (especially essays)
- The receipt of poor grades on a test, though the test material was well known by the test taker

Conversely, a person may also experience mental blocking, which involves:
- Blanking out on test questions
- Only remembering the correct answers to the questions when the test has already finished.

Fortunately for test anxiety sufferers, beating these feelings, to a large degree, has to do with proper preparation. When a test taker has a feeling of preparedness, then anxiety will be dramatically lessened.

The first step to resolving anxiety issues is to distinguish which of the two types of anxiety are being suffered. If the anxiety is a direct result of a lack of preparation, this should be considered a normal reaction, and the anxiety level (as opposed to the test results) shouldn't be anything to worry about. However, if, when adequately prepared, the test-taker still panics, blanks out, or seems to overreact, this is not a fully rational reaction. While this can be considered normal too, there are many ways to combat and overcome these effects.

Remember that anxiety cannot be entirely eliminated, however, there are ways to minimize it, to make the anxiety easier to manage. Preparation is one of the best ways to minimize test anxiety. Therefore the following techniques are wise in order to best fight off any anxiety that may want to build.

To begin with, try to avoid cramming before a test, whenever it is possible. By trying to memorize an entire term's worth of information in one day, you'll be shocking your system, and not giving yourself a very good chance to absorb the information. This is an easy path to anxiety, so for those who suffer from test anxiety, cramming should not even be considered an option.

Instead of cramming, work throughout the semester to combine all of the material which is presented throughout the semester, and work on it gradually as the course goes by, making sure to master the main concepts first, leaving minor details for a week or so before the test.

To study for the upcoming exam, be sure to pose questions that may be on the examination, to gauge the ability to answer them by integrating the ideas from your texts, notes and lectures, as well as any supplementary readings.

If it is truly impossible to cover all of the information that was covered in that particular term, concentrate on the most important portions, that can be covered very well. Learn these concepts as best as possible, so that when the test comes, a goal can be made to use these concepts as presentations of your knowledge.

In addition to study habits, changes in attitude are critical to beating a struggle with test anxiety. In fact, an improvement of the perspective over the entire test-taking experience can actually help a test taker to enjoy studying and therefore improve the overall experience. Be certain not to overemphasize the significance of the grade - know that the result of the test is neither a reflection of self worth, nor is it a measure of intelligence; one grade will not predict a person's future success.

To improve an overall testing outlook, the following steps should be tried:

- Keeping in mind that the most reasonable expectation for taking a test is to expect to try to demonstrate as much of what you know as you possibly can.
- Reminding ourselves that a test is only one test; this is not the only one, and there will be others.
- The thought of thinking of oneself in an irrational, all-or-nothing term should be avoided at all costs.
- A reward should be designated for after the test, so there's something to look forward to. Whether it be going to a movie, going out to eat, or simply visiting friends, schedule it in advance, and do it no matter what result is expected on the exam.

Test-takers should also keep in mind that the basics are some of the most important things, even beyond anti-anxiety techniques and studying. Never neglect the basic social, emotional and biological needs, in order to try to absorb information. In order to best achieve, these three factors must be held as just as important as the studying itself.

Study Steps

Remember the following important steps for studying:

- Maintain healthy nutrition and exercise habits. Continue both your recreational activities and social pass times. These both contribute to your physical and emotional well being.
- Be certain to get a good amount of sleep, especially the night before the test, because when you're overtired you are not able to perform to the best of your best ability.
- Keep the studying pace to a moderate level by taking breaks when they are needed, and varying the work whenever possible, to keep the mind fresh instead of getting bored.
- When enough studying has been done that all the material that can be learned has been learned, and the test taker is prepared for the test, stop studying and do something relaxing such as listening to music, watching a movie, or taking a warm bubble bath.

There are also many other techniques to minimize the uneasiness or apprehension that is experienced along with test anxiety before, during, or even after the examination. In fact, there are a great deal of things that can be done to stop anxiety from interfering with lifestyle and performance. Again, remember that anxiety will not be eliminated entirely, and it shouldn't be. Otherwise that "up" feeling for exams would not exist, and most of us depend on that sensation to perform better than usual. However, this anxiety has to be at a level that is manageable.

Of course, as we have just discussed, being prepared for the exam is half the battle right away. Attending all classes, finding out what knowledge will be expected on the exam, and knowing the exam schedules are easy steps to lowering anxiety. Keeping up with work will remove the need to cram, and efficient study habits will eliminate wasted time. Studying should be done in an ideal location for concentration, so that it is simple to become interested in the material and give it complete attention. A method such as

SQ3R (Survey, Question, Read, Recite, Review) is a wonderful key to follow to make sure that the study habits are as effective as possible, especially in the case of learning from a textbook. Flashcards are great techniques for memorization. Learning to take good notes will mean that notes will be full of useful information, so that less sifting will need to be done to seek out what is pertinent for studying. Reviewing notes after class and then again on occasion will keep the information fresh in the mind. From notes that have been taken summary sheets and outlines can be made for simpler reviewing.

A study group can also be a very motivational and helpful place to study, as there will be a sharing of ideas, all of the minds can work together, to make sure that everyone understands, and the studying will be made more interesting because it will be a social occasion.

Basically, though, as long as the test-taker remains organized and self confident, with efficient study habits, less time will need to be spent studying, and higher grades will be achieved.

To become self confident, there are many useful steps. The first of these is "self talk." It has been shown through extensive research, that self-talk for students who suffer from test anxiety, should be well monitored, in order to make sure that it contributes to self confidence as opposed to sinking the student. Frequently the self talk of test-anxious students is negative or self-defeating, thinking that everyone else is smarter and faster, that they always mess up, and that if they don't do well, they'll fail the entire course. It is important to decreasing anxiety that awareness is made of self talk. Try writing any negative self thoughts and then disputing them with a positive statement instead. Begin self-encouragement as though it was a friend speaking. Repeat positive statements to help reprogram the mind to believing in successes instead of failures.

Helpful Techniques

Other extremely helpful techniques include:
- Self-visualization of doing well and reaching goals
- While aiming for an "A" level of understanding, don't try to "overprotect" by setting your expectations lower. This will only convince the mind to stop studying in order to meet the lower expectations.
- Don't make comparisons with the results or habits of other students. These are individual factors, and different things work for different people, causing different results.
- Strive to become an expert in learning what works well, and what can be done in order to improve. Consider collecting this data in a journal.
- Create rewards for after studying instead of doing things before studying that will only turn into avoidance behaviors.
- Make a practice of relaxing - by using methods such as progressive relaxation, self-hypnosis, guided imagery, etc - in order to make relaxation an automatic sensation.
- Work on creating a state of relaxed concentration so that concentrating will take on the focus of the mind, so that none will be wasted on worrying.
- Take good care of the physical self by eating well and getting enough sleep.

- Plan in time for exercise and stick to this plan.

Beyond these techniques, there are other methods to be used before, during and after the test that will help the test-taker perform well in addition to overcoming anxiety.

Before the exam comes the academic preparation. This involves establishing a study schedule and beginning at least one week before the actual date of the test. By doing this, the anxiety of not having enough time to study for the test will be automatically eliminated. Moreover, this will make the studying a much more effective experience, ensuring that the learning will be an easier process. This relieves much undue pressure on the test-taker.

Summary sheets, note cards, and flash cards with the main concepts and examples of these main concepts should be prepared in advance of the actual studying time. A topic should never be eliminated from this process. By omitting a topic because it isn't expected to be on the test is only setting up the test-taker for anxiety should it actually appear on the exam. Utilize the course syllabus for laying out the topics that should be studied. Carefully go over the notes that were made in class, paying special attention to any of the issues that the professor took special care to emphasize while lecturing in class. In the textbooks, use the chapter review, or if possible, the chapter tests, to begin your review.

It may even be possible to ask the instructor what information will be covered on the exam, or what the format of the exam will be (for example, multiple choice, essay, free form, true-false). Additionally, see if it is possible to find out how many questions will be on the test. If a review sheet or sample test has been offered by the professor, make good use of it, above anything else, for the preparation for the test. Another great resource for getting to know the examination is reviewing tests from previous semesters. Use these tests to review, and aim to achieve a 100% score on each of the possible topics. With a few exceptions, the goal that you set for yourself is the highest one that you will reach.

Take all of the questions that were assigned as homework, and rework them to any other possible course material. The more problems reworked, the more skill and confidence will form as a result. When forming the solution to a problem, write out each of the steps. Don't simply do head work. By doing as many steps on paper as possible, much clarification and therefore confidence will be formed. Do this with as many homework problems as possible, before checking the answers. By checking the answer after each problem, a reinforcement will exist, that will not be on the exam. Study situations should be as exam-like as possible, to prime the test-taker's system for the experience. By waiting to check the answers at the end, a psychological advantage will be formed, to decrease the stress factor.

Another fantastic reason for not cramming is the avoidance of confusion in concepts, especially when it comes to mathematics. 8-10 hours of study will become one hundred percent more effective if it is spread out over a week or at least several days, instead of doing it all in one sitting. Recognize that the human brain requires time in order to assimilate new material, so frequent breaks and a span of study time over several days will be much more beneficial.

Additionally, don't study right up until the point of the exam. Studying should stop a minimum of one hour before the exam begins. This allows the brain to rest and put things in their proper order. This will also provide the time to become as relaxed as possible when going into the examination room. The test-taker will also have time to eat well and eat sensibly. Know that the brain needs food as much as the rest of the body. With enough food and enough sleep, as well as a relaxed attitude, the body and the mind are primed for success.

Avoid any anxious classmates who are talking about the exam. These students only spread anxiety, and are not worth sharing the anxious sentimentalities.

Before the test also involves creating a positive attitude, so mental preparation should also be a point of concentration. There are many keys to creating a positive attitude. Should fears become rushing in, make a visualization of taking the exam, doing well, and seeing an A written on the paper. Write out a list of affirmations that will bring a feeling of confidence, such as "I am doing well in my English class," "I studied well and know my material," "I enjoy this class." Even if the affirmations aren't believed at first, it sends a positive message to the subconscious which will result in an alteration of the overall belief system, which is the system that creates reality.

If a sensation of panic begins, work with the fear and imagine the very worst! Work through the entire scenario of not passing the test, failing the entire course, and dropping out of school, followed by not getting a job, and pushing a shopping cart through the dark alley where you'll live. This will place things into perspective! Then, practice deep breathing and create a visualization of the opposite situation - achieving an "A" on the exam, passing the entire course, receiving the degree at a graduation ceremony.

On the day of the test, there are many things to be done to ensure the best results, as well as the most calm outlook. The following stages are suggested in order to maximize test-taking potential:
- Begin the examination day with a moderate breakfast, and avoid any coffee or beverages with caffeine if the test taker is prone to jitters. Even people who are used to managing caffeine can feel jittery or light-headed when it is taken on a test day.
- Attempt to do something that is relaxing before the examination begins. As last minute cramming clouds the mastering of overall concepts, it is better to use this time to create a calming outlook.
- Be certain to arrive at the test location well in advance, in order to provide time to select a location that is away from doors, windows and other distractions, as well as giving enough time to relax before the test begins.
- Keep away from anxiety generating classmates who will upset the sensation of stability and relaxation that is being attempted before the exam.
- Should the waiting period before the exam begins cause anxiety, create a self-distraction by reading a light magazine or something else that is relaxing and simple.

During the exam itself, read the entire exam from beginning to end, and find out how much time should be allotted to each individual problem. Once writing the exam, should more time be taken for a problem, it should be abandoned, in order to begin another problem. If there is time at the end, the unfinished problem can always be returned to and completed.

Read the instructions very carefully - twice - so that unpleasant surprises won't follow during or after the exam has ended.

When writing the exam, pretend that the situation is actually simply the completion of homework within a library, or at home. This will assist in forming a relaxed atmosphere, and will allow the brain extra focus for the complex thinking function.

Begin the exam with all of the questions with which the most confidence is felt. This will build the confidence level regarding the entire exam and will begin a quality momentum. This will also create encouragement for trying the problems where uncertainty resides.

Going with the "gut instinct" is always the way to go when solving a problem. Second guessing should be avoided at all costs. Have confidence in the ability to do well.

For essay questions, create an outline in advance that will keep the mind organized and make certain that all of the points are remembered. For multiple choice, read every answer, even if the correct one has been spotted - a better one may exist.

Continue at a pace that is reasonable and not rushed, in order to be able to work carefully. Provide enough time to go over the answers at the end, to check for small errors that can be corrected.

Should a feeling of panic begin, breathe deeply, and think of the feeling of the body releasing sand through its pores. Visualize a calm, peaceful place, and include all of the sights, sounds and sensations of this image. Continue the deep breathing, and take a few minutes to continue this with closed eyes. When all is well again, return to the test.

If a "blanking" occurs for a certain question, skip it and move on to the next question. There will be time to return to the other question later. Get everything done that can be done, first, to guarantee all the grades that can be compiled, and to build all of the confidence possible. Then return to the weaker questions to build the marks from there.

Remember, one's own reality can be created, so as long as the belief is there, success will follow. And remember: anxiety can happen later, right now, there's an exam to be written!

After the examination is complete, whether there is a feeling for a good grade or a bad grade, don't dwell on the exam, and be certain to follow through on the reward that was promised…and enjoy it! Don't dwell on any mistakes that have been made, as there is nothing that can be done at this point anyway.

Additionally, don't begin to study for the next test right away. Do something relaxing for a while, and let the mind relax and prepare itself to begin absorbing information again.

From the results of the exam - both the grade and the entire experience, be certain to learn from what has gone on. Perfect studying habits and work some more on confidence in order to make the next examination experience even better than the last one.

Learn to avoid places where openings occurred for laziness, procrastination and day dreaming.

Use the time between this exam and the next one to better learn to relax, even learning to relax on cue, so that any anxiety can be controlled during the next exam. Learn how to relax the body. Slouch in your chair if that helps. Tighten and then relax all of the different muscle groups, one group at a time, beginning with the feet and then working all the way up to the neck and face. This will ultimately relax the muscles more than they were to begin with. Learn how to breathe deeply and comfortably, and focus on this breathing going in and out as a relaxing thought. With every exhale, repeat the word "relax."

As common as test anxiety is, it is very possible to overcome it. Make yourself one of the test-takers who overcome this frustrating hindrance.

Additional Bonus Material

Due to our efforts to try to keep this book to a manageable length, we've created a link that will give you access to all of your additional bonus material.

Please visit http://www.mometrix.com/bonus948/dsstethicsamer to access the information.